C000182200

ADVENTUROUS PUB WALKS
IN
THE PEAK DISTRICT

Charles Wildgoose

COUNTRYSIDE BOOKS
NEWBURY BERKSHIRE

First published 2004
© Charles Wildgoose 2004

All rights reserved. No reproduction
permitted without the prior permission
of the publisher:

COUNTRYSIDE BOOKS
3 Catherine Road
Newbury, Berkshire

To view our complete range of books,
please visit us at
www.countrysidebooks.co.uk

ISBN 1 85306 848 9

Designed by Peter Davies, Nautilus Design
Photographs by the author

Produced through MRM Associates Ltd., Reading
Typeset by Techniset Typesetters, Newton-le-Willows
Printed by Woolnough Bookbinding Ltd., Irthlingborough

CONTENTS

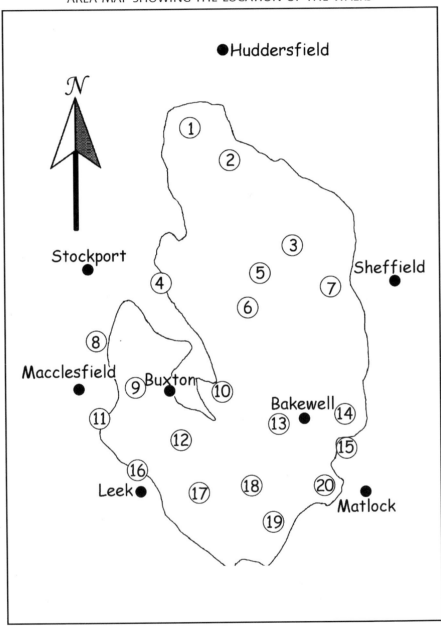

INTRODUCTION

In this book you get the opportunity to enjoy some of the best landscapes in the Peak District, if not the country. Many of the views are staggering. It's not just the fantastic scenery you'll be able to enjoy though – you will also see the impact man has had on this area. Okay, there may be a few too many quarries in and around the Peak District but, as many people will tell you, there is a need to provide work for the residents (of which I'm one) and, of course, to a great extent it is man who has managed and crafted the countryside that you will be walking through.

As you follow these walks, you will see impressive examples of man's engineering skills – various dams (including Ladybower), the Tissington and High Peak Trails (both formerly railway lines), the Macclesfield Canal and many, many fascinating buildings. But it is the countryside that will really grip you.

Be prepared to walk a bit further with these walks! They are all between 8 and 12¾ miles in length and, if you've never tackled 8 miles before, try one of the shorter routes first. Go well prepared. Ideally, you should have waterproof gear with you because if you are caught out in a storm in the middle of nowhere you will know about it. Have the appropriate OS map handy as well. The walks have all been checked but things can change in the countryside and we don't want you getting lost because a hedge has disappeared.

There are some amazing pubs to visit but they can be busy so do allow enough time to get to the pub, eat *and* get back to the car. Personally, I would try and be at the pub when it opens (or soon after). Then you should be sure of finding a seat and getting away in good time to finish the walk. The telephone numbers of the pubs are given so you can check whether they're open on a particular day or whether they're likely to be busy.

Remember to take off your boots when entering the pub or wear something over them (some walkers use plastic bags for this and I understand you can buy special plastic boot covers, too). The main thing is to make sure, please, that you don't wear big, muddy boots on the plush carpet of the pub – you wouldn't like it if someone did this in your front room, would you?

It's always good to know how people get on with these walks so feel free to contact me on my e-mail address – wildgoose@zetnet.co.uk – I'll look forward to hearing from you.

In the meantime, enjoy your walking.

Charles Wildgoose

ACKNOWLEDGEMENTS

Once again, I wish to thank everyone who helped by checking these walks. In no particular order, I would like to thank Alex Pryor and Sharon Price, Richard Roberts and Kathryn Weeks, Ron and Elizabeth Haydock, Louis McMeeken and Christine (as well as the collies, Boris and Josey), Di Carnell, Ruth and Graham Rhodes, Amanda Wardman, Kath Walker, Julian Elliott, Paul Hopkins and Bob Davies, Martin Pape, George Wolfe and Rosemary Wolfe, Peter Thompson and last, but not least, Ian Swindell.

Valuable contributions were also made by Martin Harris, of Severn-Trent Water; Mick Hanson, of Sheffield City Council; and Gordon Danks, of the Peak National Park; as well as H.J. Enthovens. A special word of thanks goes to Paul Hopkins, Peak Park Rights of Way Officer, who had to field quite a few moans and groans from me about various decrepit stiles that I encountered on the walks.

Finally, as always, I have to give special mention to Balkees who was unable to weigh in with her usual contribution this time round. However, I am still thankful for what she has done and for her moral support, too.

PUBLISHER'S NOTE

*W*e hope that you obtain considerable enjoyment from this book; great care has been taken in its preparation. Although at the time of publication all routes followed public rights of way or permitted paths, diversion orders can be made and permissions withdrawn.

We cannot, of course, be held responsible for such diversion orders and any inaccuracies in the text which result from these or any other changes to the routes nor any damage which might result from walkers trespassing on private property. We are anxious though that all details covering the walks are kept up to date and would therefore welcome information from readers which would be relevant to future editions.

The simple sketch maps that accompany the walks in this book are based on notes made by the author whilst checking out the routes on the ground. They are designed to show you how to reach the start, to point out the main features of the overall circuit and they contain a progression of numbers that relate to the paragraphs of the text.

However, for the benefit of a proper map, we do recommend that you purchase the relevant Ordnance Survey sheet covering your walk. The Ordnance Survey maps are widely available, especially through booksellers and local newsagents.

DIGLEY RESERVOIR, THE HOLME VALLEY AND HOLME

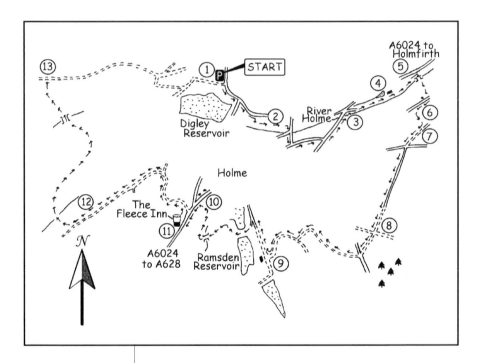

Distance:
11¹/₂ miles
(pub is visited after 7 miles)

Starting point:
The Digley Quarry car park.
GR 110073

Map: OS Outdoor Leisure 1 The Peak District – Dark Peak Area

How to get there: *Take the A6024 through Holme, to the south-west of Holmfirth. Turn north along Fieldhead Lane. Park in the quarry car park on the **northern** side of Digley Reservoir.*

LOOKING EASTWARDS FROM CARTWORTH MOOR ROAD

*D*on't tell anyone but half of this walk is outside the Peak District ... and you would probably be hard pressed to work out which bit. This is *Last of the Summer Wine* country, of course, and if you're a fan you may very well recognise one or two places, possibly more. There's a great variety of scenery on this route, which takes you south of Holmfirth and over the Ramsden Reservoir to a lunch stop at a terrific pub just over halfway round.

Be prepared to really enjoy visiting the **Fleece Inn** at Holme, but watch out you don't sit on the cat near the fireplace. There's a good view and splendid beer and a nice feel to it. Remember, though, that they close on Mondays (except bank holidays); otherwise they open on Tuesday to Friday from 12 noon until 3 pm and 6 pm until 11 pm. They open from 12 noon at the weekend until 11 pm on Saturdays and 10.30 pm on Sundays. Food is served from 12 noon until 2 pm and 6 pm until 9 pm. The Fleece does get busy so try and arrive in good time to claim a table.

There's a good variety of things to eat, with hot and cold sandwiches, vegetarian meals, and a specials board listing dishes such as steaks or monkfish. As regards beer the regular is Burtonwood Bitter with guests which change monthly such as Top Hat Premium Ale or Jennings Cumberland Ale.

Telephone: *01484 683449.*

The Walk

① From the car park, walk back to the entrance and turn right (there is a path on the right avoiding the road if you wish). About 250 yards later, ignore the road across the reservoir wall to the right. Continue forward downhill, bearing right. Pass through a kissing gate on the right to follow the **Holme Valley Riverside Way**, initially with the road immediately to your left. The path descends diagonally through the trees. At the bottom is a tarmac lane which you should turn left along. The **River Holme** is down to your right. (¹/₂ mile)

The river Holme is only eight miles long, starting just below the TV mast and Holme Moss, and continuing through Holmfirth until it reaches the River Colne.

② As you leave the trees, you may catch a glimpse of **St David's church** at **Holmbridge** ahead. Turn right at the road by the church. Fork left over the river into **Bank Lane**.

Then left into **Smithy Lane**. This rises to become **Dobb Top Road**. Ignore roads to the right. Some of the cottages here are delightful. On joining **Dobb Lane**, bear left downhill. At the bottom of the hill (with three-storey houses all around) cross the bridge. (1 mile)

There used to be thirteen mills between Digley and Holmfirth, where men, women and children all worked. One of the mills lies beneath the reservoir near the car park. Like so many northern towns it was weaving and mills that resulted in the growth of Holmfirth. One claim to fame that Holmfirth has (in addition to 'The Last of the Summer Wine') is that Bamforth's postcards used to be produced there. They were the saucy seaside cards that were so popular when I was a lad.

③ With **Old Road** turning sharp left, bear right into **Water Street**. This takes you alongside a delightful row of cottages. Beyond them ignore the footbridge to the right. Walk downstream, with the river to your right. You will soon be walking between the river and a canalised watercourse. Keep on the right side of a millpond, with a tall redbrick chimney at the far end. ($^1/_4$ mile)

④ When you reach the chimney, turn sharp right and head towards a footbridge. Just 15 yards before it, turn left and follow the river again. This path runs alongside the remains of a mill on your left and the river on your right. Stay beside the river all the way to the main road. ($^1/_4$ mile)

⑤ Turn right at the road, then right over the bridge opposite the **Victoria Inn**. Walk forward away from the road through a squeeze-stile. Head up to the trees slightly right and ahead of you. Pass through the squeeze-stile on the left side of the trees. Walk up through the trees, climb a few grassy steps and walk up the right side of the wall to the lane at the top. ($^1/_4$ mile)

⑥ There's a good view here of the **Holme Valley**. Turn right, noticing the '1752' date on the old building on your right. **Holme Moss mast** should be ahead of you. About 200 yards later, just before the right turn to **Malkin House**, take the footpath up the steps on your left. Walk up the left side of the field. At the wall corner, bear half left to a stile. From

WATER STREET NEAR HOLMFIRTH

11

there, bear left towards another stile just above the tumbled-down stone outbuilding. ($^1/_4$ mile)

⑦ Turn right at the stony track. There are marvellous views of the patchwork quilt of fields from here. At the old quarry on the left, fork left uphill. At the crossroads keep forward along **Cartworth Moor Road**. On the right is what must be one of the highest cricket grounds in the country. The crossroads is just under 1,000 feet above sea level. Walk just over $^1/_2$ mile on this road until it fizzles out into a stony track, and 500 yards later you reach another crossroads. If you turn left here you will get the chance to visit **Elysium** as well as **Hades**! ($1^1/_2$ miles)

Elysium and Hades being Heaven and Hell in Greek mythology, there must be a reason for calling two properties this! At the time of writing I haven't found it. If anyone knows the reason, perhaps they could get in touch!

⑧ Take the 'safe' option and keep straight forward. You then reach another crossroads. Ignoring the road to left and right, take the track opposite. Stay on this for $^2/_3$ mile. It then swings left and downhill; 450 yards later follow it round to the right and downhill. Stay on it as it subsequently swings left and into the trees. You come

out in front of **Ramsden House**. ($1^3/_4$ miles)

⑨ Turn right along the track signed **'Kirklees Way'**.

The Kirklees Way is a circular route, 72 miles long, full of interesting scenery. It can be tackled in one go or split into a number of day walks.

After 100 yards, **Ramsden Reservoir** appears to your left. Pass a car park to your right and proceed along the walled lane ahead for 150 yards, then take a sharp left and follow the path across the reservoir wall. The path bears right uphill on the far side of the reservoir. Ignore a footpath sharp left as you proceed. Your path continues to rise a little, then swings left beside a fence. The mast of **Holme Moss** is to your left. The path descends to cross **Rake Dike**, bearing right beyond. Cross a step-over into a field and head diagonally across this into the far top corner. Turn left immediately between wall and fence. Pass through a gate, switching onto the other side of the wall, keeping in the same direction though. Keep forward to the road. (1 mile)

⑩ Turn left into **Holme**, passing the **Old School**. Ignore **Fieldhead Lane** to the right. Continue forward to the pub on the right. ($^1/_4$ mile)

⑪ After lunch, turn left. Turn left again at the cobbled area and proceed towards the playground with a 1686 date. Keep to the right of this, walking up **Meal Hill Road**. Stay on this to reach **The Nook** on your left. Ignore the path to the right. Stay on the tarmac lane, passing the **Old Schoolroom** dated 1880. The lane becomes stonier. Pass a farmhouse on the right. Where the track splits, take the left fork. After 500 yards it splits again. This time ignore the left fork, keeping straight forward (signed 'No Bikes Footpath Only'). (1½ miles)

⑫ At the end of the walled track, you enter open ground. Keep forward for nearly 500 yards, then fork right off the track you're on, just before a 'bump' in the ground. The path swings right fairly quickly so you're heading into a valley, with a stream to your left. Cross this, following the path alongside a wall initially. The path then rises over the moorside, swinging left and descending into the next valley. Cross the footbridge just below the confluence of two streams. Rise up to the right on a walled path and

20 yards later turn sharp left uphill. The track you're on brings you to a gate. Cross the stile and walk alongside the tumbled-down wall on your left to reach a green lane. (1½ miles)

⑬ Turn right here (it's called **Nether Lane**) and descend gradually. As you go, ignore any paths to the left. Just under a mile after joining the lane, follow the **Kirklees Way** down a track on the right. This leads downhill, with **Bilberry Reservoir** on your right below. On reaching a point where another path joins from sharp right, ignore this, keeping straight forward. Stay on this track all the way back to the quarry car park. (1½ miles)

In the mid-19th century the original Bilberry Reservoir burst. Over 80 people downstream were drowned and houses and other buildings damaged. Just a few years later, the same thing happened again at Bradfield. This time over three times as many people died.

Date walk completed:

LANGSETT RESERVOIR WOODS TO DUNFORD BRIDGE

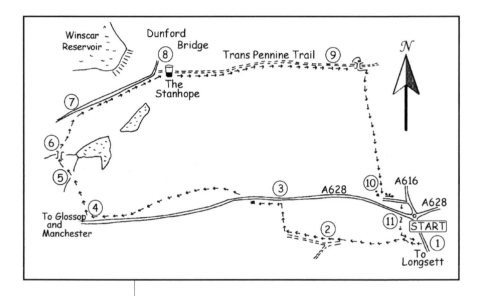

Distance:
9 miles
(visit the Stanhope
after 5¼ miles)
Starting point:
Flouch car park.
GR 201012

Map: OS Outdoor Leisure 1 The Peak District – Dark Peak Area

How to get there: Flouch car park is 400 yards
south-east of the roundabout where the A616 crosses
the A628 north-west of Langsett.

GOING NORTH ALONG THE ROUTE FROM THE A628 TO WINDLEDEN

A bracing walk with a real surprise about halfway round – the pub. It's like no other pub I've visited in the seven books I've written. The food is sublime and the welcome genuine. The walk itself? It's an interesting mix of exposed moorland and an easier second half along the Trans Pennine Trail.

View the **Stanhope** at Dunford Bridge from the outside and what do you see? A solid stone-built pub with nothing particularly unusual about it. Once you enter you're in for a shock – a very pleasant one I hasten to add. When I first entered, I felt out of place – surely they don't want people like me in here – y'know 'walkers'. How wrong can you be! I was made to feel most welcome and have enjoyed every visit since.

The food is sublime with the chicken tagliatelle and the home-made chicken and black pudding sausages being a couple of the dishes I can vouch for. The sweets are excellent too. Timothy Taylor Landlord and Black Sheep Bitter are on offer, together with various other forms of liquid refreshment.

15

As for opening times, in winter, on Saturday they're open from 12 noon until 11 pm and on Sunday from 12 noon until 11 pm. Weekdays it's 6 pm until 11 pm. Food is served on Saturday from 12 noon until 2 pm (then from 7 pm until 9 pm) and on Sunday from 12 noon until 4.30 pm. Midweek it's 7 pm until 9 pm. In summertime (and you may need to check with the pub on this), the Stanhope hopes to stay open all day from midday, seven days a week. Food will be available at the weekend but it may be best to contact them to find out the exact midweek position.

Telephone: *01226 763104 or visit the website www.thestanhopearms.co.uk where you can get more up to date information.*

The Walk

① Leave the car park at the end furthest from the roundabout. Cross the A616. Follow the bridleway heading away from the road. This gravel track bends right, then left. The bridleway forks 450 yards later. Take the right fork. After no more than 10 yards, though, ignore a subsequent bridleway to the right. Keep forward, passing between walls before crossing over a stream. The bridleway levels out and passes under an avenue of oak trees. A bridlegate takes you out of **Langsett Reservoir Woods**. Proceed, with an open field on your right. Pass through another gate and 30 yards later turn right along a bridleway between walls, ignoring a footpath on your right almost immediately. On reaching a pair of gateways, pass through the one on the left. (1 mile)

② After 100 yards, turn right along the bridleway known as **Swinden Lane**. Keep on this for 800 yards, crossing the driveway to an isolated property to your left as you do so. On reaching open countryside, walk forward a few yards, then turn right along a grassy track. After 60 yards, join a more defined track. Keep forward along this, with a wall on your right. No sooner have you entered open country than you're leaving it. Keep forward to the main road. ($^3/_4$ mile)

③ Turn left to reach the **Dog & Partridge**, 450 yards later. Just beyond this, fork onto the moorland and follow a moorland track.

This is referred to as 'Snow Road' on the OS map, though it's not clear whether this is its name or a description of what it is. As you proceed, though, you'll see a wicket-fence on your left to keep the snow off the main road so it may be the latter.

This old moorland road you're on climbs steadily across the moor.

You'll probably hear the 'Go-back go-back' call of red grouse that frequent this moor. You'll also see, in autumn, some vibrantly coloured scarlet and orange grasses.

Just over a mile after joining it, the track draws nearer to the A628. Continue on the track until you reach the gate leading onto the road. Don't pass through this, keep to the right of it and walk alongside the wicket fence, which is now on your right. Pass over the bridge made of railway sleepers. The litter around a layby indicates that you're nearer 'civilisation'. Just beyond the layby, pass through a bridlegate. (1³/₄ miles)

④ Then, just when you feel you can't take any more roadside walking, a bridlegate on your right gets you away from the road. Take heed: at the time of writing a notice here reads 'This footpath can be very boggy during wet weather'. Whether this applies to the path

MILESTONE BESIDE THE OLD MANCHESTER ROAD

you've just walked or the bridleway you're going to walk is unclear because of the angle the notice is set at! With this in mind press on, following the clear bridleway ahead. As you proceed you'll see **Upper Windleden Reservoir**, with **Winscar Reservoir** beyond that. With almost every step the noise of the road behind declines. If you're in mist hereabouts, you should be okay and able to follow the bridleway. If not, then just keep descending. The bridleway crosses a stream. ($^{1}/_{2}$ mile)

⑤ The bridleway levels out. As you proceed alongside a wall on your right, do not keep forward to pass through the gateway in front – bear left to reach a gate some 70 yards to the left of the gateway ahead. Follow the clear path beyond the gate. This descends fairly quickly into a valley, with the reservoir to your right. ($^{1}/_{4}$ mile)

⑥ Cross a bridge and rise up the other side. As you proceed, the path starts to bend left. Walk alongside a metal fence on your right. At the corner of the fence, veer away from it into the valley beyond. Cross another footbridge and ascend the hillside ahead. The path bears right towards **Windleden** (the farm above the reservoir) before swinging left. It can get boggy here. The path meanders uphill to a metal

bridlegate, with a lane beyond. ($^{1}/_{4}$ mile)

⑦ Turn right down the lane for $^{3}/_{4}$ mile into **Dunford Bridge**. The **Stanhope** is on your right. ($^{3}/_{4}$ mile)

⑧ Lunch done, come out of the **Stanhope's** car park and turn sharp right to follow the **Upper Don Trail**, which forms part of the **Trans Pennine Trail**. Keep forward, with a high wall on your right, to negotiate various 'barriers', which presumably are intended to deter illegal use of the Trail. Join the main route of the Trail, bearing right beneath the pylons.

It seems walkers are encouraged to walk on the left-hand side of the Trail and horseriders the right. There are some interesting seats along the way.

After being hemmed in a little, the Trail opens out on the right so you get views of the moorland. ($1^{3}/_{4}$ miles)

The Trans Pennine Trail is a route that stretches from Southport on the west coast of England all the way across to Hornsea on the east. In between there are various links with places as diverse as Leeds, York and Chesterfield. I have even seen a sign on the Chesterfield Canal indicating Chesterfield one way and Istanbul the other – the reason being that a long distance route is planned to run all the way through Europe into Turkey. If you start walking now, it may be open by the time you get there.

⑨ After passing a seat indicating that **Penistone** is 6km ahead, you will reach a bridge across the Trail. Immediately before it, climb the steps on the left and cross it. Beyond it turn left and 40 yards later turn right through a gate to walk alongside a wall on your left. Stay beside the wall for $^1/_2$ mile before walking a further $^1/_4$ mile between walls. (1 mile)

⑩ Keep forward between the properties to turn left along **Old Manchester Road**. Look out for an old milepost after 350 yards, then 100 yards later take the footpath to the left of the bridleway, marked by

the **Peak & Northern Footpaths** sign for the **Derwent Valley** via **Cut Gate** and **Slippery Stones**. The footpath joins the bridleway. Keep forward to the road. ($^1/_2$ mile)

The Peak & Northern Footpaths Society is the 'oldest outdoor amenities organisation in the country' according to their website. They have erected over 300 footpath signposts and continue to do so to this day.

⑪ Cross the A628 carefully. Proceed on the bridleway beyond, descending to the left, then bearing right, into the trees. Stay on it for just under 400 yards as it swings back to your outward route. When you reach this, turn left back to the car park. ($^1/_2$ mile)

Date walk completed:

STRINES MOOR, AGDEN RESERVOIR AND HIGH BRADFIELD

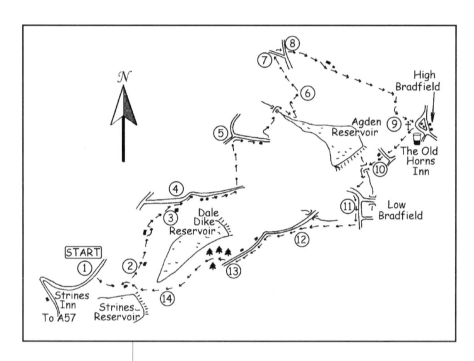

Distance:
8¹/₂ miles
(visit the Old
Horns Inn after
5¹/₄ miles)

Starting point:
Roadside parking
north of the Strines
Inn. GR 226909

Map: OS Outdoor Leisure 1 The Peak District – Dark Peak Area

How to get there: *Head north from the A57 west of Sheffield for Strines Moor, passing the Strines Inn. Continue for ³/₄ mile beyond the inn and park on the right-hand side of the road. (If there's no space, then park nearer to the inn. This will mean some road-walking to get to the start.)*

HIGH BRADFIELD CEMETERY

A wonderful area full of good views, initially of the reservoirs. Then you reach High Bradfield and its fascinating church. One of the tombstones, in the path leading to the church door, reads 'Here lieth the Body of Joseph Beaver who died' – that's all! The walk descends to Low Bradfield where you can feed the ducks. The return to the car runs along the other side of the reservoirs.

It's funny how you're not aware of some pubs until you have to find one for a walk. This is how it was for me with the **Old Horns Inn** at High Bradfield. There's usually something different about a pub when people queue outside before opening time. Well, it may have something to do with the excellent three-course Economy Lunch that's available on Tuesday and Thursday! Mind you, the food is good at any time with dishes such as scampi, honey roast duck, spicy lamb casserole, jacket potatoes and a host of sandwiches. The beers are all Thwaites: Lancaster Bomber, Cask Thoroughbred, Cask Original, Dark Mild and Premium Smooth.

Food is served from 12 noon until 2 pm and 5.30 pm to 9 pm on Monday to Saturday and from 12 noon until 2 pm and 5.30 pm to 8 pm on Sunday. Opening times are longer, of course.

Telephone: *0114 285 1207.*

The Walk

① Walk down the bridleway for **Broggin House**. Beyond **Strines Reservoir** on your right, **Boot's Folly** should be easily visible. After 500 yards you reach **Broggin House**. Keep left of this alongside the plantation on your left. (1/2 mile)

Boot's Folly was built in the 1920s by Charles Boot's workers. Because work was slow he occupied them by getting them to build the tower.

② After 300 yards, you reach **Stubbin Farm**. Walk past this on your right to enter an open field. Keep forward with the wall on your left. Pass through a gateway, now with the wall on your right.

Two and half miles ahead is a long quarry face with High Bradfield to the right of it.

Ignore a couple of gateways to the right. Walk towards **Hallfield** ahead. Pass through a gate directly in front and walk between the wall on your right and the fence on your left. The bridleway passes through a gate, keeping to the right of the house to reach the far side (alternatively, you could use the permissive footpath to the right of the property). Follow the track away from **Hallfield** and pass through a gateway. Having passed a stone outbuilding on your right, continue along the track between walls ahead. There's a good view of **Dale Dike Reservoir** from here. (3/4 mile)

The original Dale Dike Dam was the source of the worst ever dam disaster in England. In 1864 it burst its banks sending millions of gallons of water down the Loxley Valley. Over 240 people died that night.

③ Continue for 350 yards and, with a farm ahead, fork left through the middle gateway to ascend the bridleway beyond. Pass through two more gates to a lane. (1/4 mile)

④ Turn right and 500 yards later pass some properties on the right. After 200 yards, ignore a path on the right to **Dale Dike Reservoir**.

After a further 80 yards, turn left up another bridleway. Enter the field beyond a gate. Walk up the left side, up the hollow-way. At the end of the first field on the left ignore the sunken lane between parallel walls; keep to the right of it. Beyond this, with a gap leading into the third field on your left, keep straight forward uphill and pass a prominent white post, still with a wall to your left. Pass through a gate. Continue up the bridleway to a road. (1 mile)

⑤ Turn right and right again after 60 yards. Descend the lane, passing **Wilkin Hill Outdoor Centre**. After 100 yards, take the path on the left into delightful **Windy Bank Wood**, and 50 yards later swing left between walls. Cross a stream, swinging right beyond. At the edge of the clearing, there's a path to the right and one to the left, to the

ruins of **Agden House**. Ignore them, continuing forward. This takes you between some old gateposts. Descend, gently, into the valley. Cross a stone bridge over **Agden Dike**. This brings you to **Agden Bog**, a nature reserve, important for its 'acid mire community and associated flora and fauna'. Beyond the bridge swing right between the bog on your left and the dike on your right. After 300 yards, pass through a gateway, turning sharp left beside a wall on your left. Within 200 yards the path bears right, climbing steeply up **Agden Side**, with a plantation on your right, and 100 yards later you cross onto the other side of the wall, continuing uphill. (1 mile)

⑥ At the top of the bank, turn left alongside a wall on your right. Partway along the path a seat in memory of Anthony George Lilly

FEEDING THE DUCKS AT LOW BRADFIELD

provides a chance to enjoy the view and the words on the plaque there. Press on beside the wall. Cross a stile and turn right up to the lane. (¹/₂ mile)

⑦ Cross the lane and the stile beyond. Walk to the path ahead. Turn right to cross a stile bringing you to another lane.

⑧ Cross this lane and the stile beyond. Walk down the walled track as it bears right, all the way to the ruins of **Rocher Head**. Keep on the right side of the ruined farmbuildings, past the pigsties and a large water trough. Swing right through a gateway. Turn left beyond, alongside the wall on your left, and keep forward. Walk beside a line of hawthorns on your right. Keep in the same direction beside a 'drop' on your right. Eventually, towards the end of the field, cross a ladder-stile on your right, ignoring another to your left. Beyond the stile, turn left beside a fence. When it ends keep forward towards the 5 yards stretch of wall ahead. Cross the stile in this. Beyond bear right along the obvious path. **Agden Reservoir** is down to your right. Walk for 250 yards through this field and pass through a gateway. Turn right downhill to another gateway 20 yards later. Turn left along the walled path. Stay on this to reach a stream. Cross this and pass through the kissing gate beyond. Walk

directly up the path through the dark woodland. Pass through a small gateway, turning right. Stay on this path to reach **Bradfield churchyard** 350 yards later. Follow the path through the graveyard, past the church on your right, to reach **Jane Street**. Turn right past the **Watch House**. Turn left to the **Old Horns Inn**. (1¹/₄ miles)

The Watch House was built to keep an eye out for bodysnatchers. Hard to believe that there used to be a need to watch for such activities.

⑨ After lunch return to the **Watch House**. Turn left down the path in front of the church gates. Bear right in front of the church. Pass through a small gate and 15 yards later pass through another, larger gate, walking alongside the wall on your left. Pass through another gateway, keeping beside a wall on your right. Go through the gap at the end of the field, descending alongside the oak trees on your left. This takes you alongside a wall on your left. Keep descending and cross a stile to reach the lane. (¹/₄ mile)

⑩ Go down the path on the left side of the property. Cross the bridge at the bottom. Turn left alongside the stream. Ignore another bridge on your left. Continue forward along the paved path away from the stream. Swing left along the tarmac road to reach a grass triangle. Turn left to reach **Fair House Lane**. Ignore **Smithy Bridge Road** to the left to enter **Mill Lee Road**. (¹/₄ mile)

Bradfield parish is the largest in England and has over 110 miles of paths.

⑪ Proceed uphill, ignoring the left turn for **Dungworth**, and 20 yards later turn right along a track, taking you past a house on your right after 300 yards. Continue along the track beyond. Cross a stile by a gate. Continue along the path, ignoring a gate to your left. Cross another stile, keeping forward with a stream to your right. At the end of the field, climb a stile onto the lane. (¹/₂ mile)

⑫ Turn left, ignoring a driveway on the left almost immediately. Keep on the lane for some distance. Ignore the private road to the right. Climb the lane, passing **Blindside Cottage** on your right. Pass another property on your right and 300 yards after this follow the path on your right into the plantation. (³/₄ mile)

⑬ Follow the path/track into **Wragg**

House Plantation and 200 yards later (where the path forks) keep forward, ignoring the right fork. **Boot's Folly** should be visible as you reach the edge of the wood. Continue into the field and 50 yards later, bear right downhill along a track. Keep forward in the second field towards the Folly. Enter some rougher ground. This is **Andrew Wood**, managed under a Countryside Stewardship Scheme. Bear right down to a stile. Cross the field beyond, passing through a pair of redundant gateposts before walking beside a line of trees on your left. Pass through a stile into **Holes Wood**. Cross the stream. Rise up to and climb a stile by a gate. (³/₄ mile)

⑭ Proceed alongside the wall on your right to reach a stile. Climb this, bearing left beyond, initially with a stream on your right. Cross the open ground to a bridge, ignoring another to your right. Enter the plantation, ascending the path ahead. Pass a wall corner on your right, aiming for the house ahead. Climb another stile and rise up to **Broggin House**. Keep right of this before bearing left behind it along the drive you walked earlier. Return to your car. (³/₄ mile)

Date walk completed:

HAYFIELD, THE SNAKE PATH AND ROWARTH

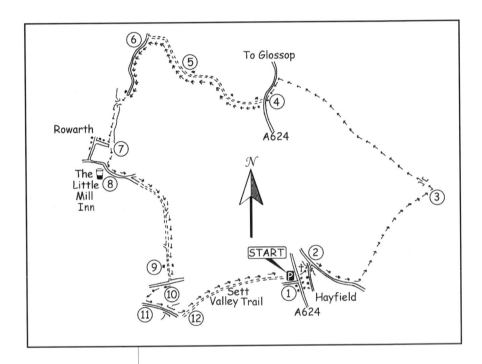

Distance:
8¹/₂ miles
(visit the Little
Mill Inn after
5¹/₂ miles)

Starting point:
*The car park at
Hayfield Visitor
Centre. GR 036869*

Map: OS Outdoor Leisure 1 The Peak District – Dark Peak Area

How to get there: *Hayfield is south of Glossop on the
A624. The car park is on the western side of this road in
the village.*

THE SNAKE PATH LEADING TOWARDS THE SHOOTING CABIN

*T*here are spectacular views as you climb the Snake Path out of Hayfield. It may be a bit of a climb but this will give you the chance to enjoy the views. Just when you think Kinder Scout is beckoning, the walk swings left and you slowly descend back to the main road, the A624. You're soon beyond that and walking through the interesting scenery which leads to a most marvellous lunch stop – the Little Mill Inn. After some enjoyable food an old track leads you back towards Hayfield before a steady (and flat) mile or so returns you to the car park at Hayfield.

The **Little Mill Inn** is well off the beaten track and yet it's sought out by so many people that it must be doing something right. It's quirky, charming and full of character, as you will discover – and since it's on your route through Rowarth, *you* won't have to go looking for it.

The food is tasty and wholesome. Who wouldn't be tempted by the sound of

Bury black pudding, lamb madras, rogan josh, king burger or barbecued ribs? My mouth is watering just typing this. Then there are specials such as peppered steak. Banks's Bitter and Marston's Pedigree are always available plus a couple of ever-changing guests, usually from Robinsons, Slaters, Coach House or Phoenix Breweries. The inn is open every day from 12 noon.

Telephone: *01663 743178.*

 *The Walk*

① Cross the main road from the car park via the pelican crossing. Walk down the right side of the church and turn left over the roadbridge. Immediately beyond, turn right towards the **Royal Hotel**. Walk up the cobbled lane to the left of it (signed 'To **Kinder**'). (¹/₄ mile)

② Turn right on **Kinder Road**. Stay on this for 300 yards to reach house number 121. Turn left up the **Kinder-Snake Inn path**. Pass through a gate then another. As you climb there are good views of **Hayfield** down to your left. Pass through a kissing gate by a bridlegate and walk up to the far top corner of the field ahead. Pass through another kissing gate by a bridlegate. Then, pass through a third such kissing gate to enter rougher ground. The bridleway now runs beside a wall on your left towards the moorland ahead. Enter the moorland through a farmgate where you'll spot a National Trust

'**Snake Path**' sign. Head towards the shooting cabin. To the right, you may catch a glimpse of **Kinder Downfall**, a waterfall that carries the waters of the **River Kinder** over the edge of the plateau. Ignore a path sharp left after 100 yards. (1¹/₂ miles)

The Snake Path runs for six miles across the moorland between Hayfield and the Snake Inn on the Snake Pass Road.

③ With the cabin 100 yards ahead, turn left along the footpath signed '**Glossop** via **Car Meadow**'. Cross a long, low, wooden footbridge. After subsequently going over a stream, ignore a track crossing the bridleway. Keep forward with the valley on your left. For some way, you'll be walking alongside a high stone wall on your left. The path then descends steadily towards the main road ahead. On reaching **Hollingworth Clough**, cross a bridge. Bear left to a gate. Turn left on the main road for 500 yards. Take care here, avoiding the inside of any bends. (1 mile)

④ Turn right down **Lanehead Road**. This tarmac lane takes you through the properties at **Brookhouses**. Stay on the lane as it climbs fairly steeply. There are good views to the left and behind. Pass **Stet Barn Farm**. The lane gets a *bit* easier at **Lanehead Farm**. Ignore a number of footpaths on the left hereabouts. After crossing a cattle grid, ignore the path to the right; take the bridleway towards the farm ahead. Keep straight forward through the property, passing a duckpond on your right. This brings you almost immediately to a track. (1 mile)

⑤ Turn right along this for 600 yards to reach a gate. **Cown Edge** is visible ahead. As you proceed you are likely to spot some of the planes on their way to or from Manchester Airport. About 300 yards along the track (now with a moor on your right) you reach a tarmac lane. (1/2 mile)

⑥ Turn left down this. **Lantern Pike** is the highest point ahead of you. Immediately beyond **Grove House** at the bottom of the hill, bear right through the gate on the bridleway running between walls. Just beyond a ruined barn, cross a stream. Immediately after, fork left along a path with the stream on your left. Follow this clear path through the

HORSES CROSSING THE BRIDLEWAY BRIDGE NEAR THE SHOOTING CABIN

valley with the stream never that far from you. Ignore a footbridge on your left. Pass through a grove of trees to reach another footbridge. Cross this and turn right to pass through a concrete ford. Turn left over another stile with the stream still to your left. You then reach a wicket gate. Proceed into **Rowarth**. (1 mile)

At the top of the lane to your right are Drinkwater's Buildings dated 1812, a terrace of attractive cottages in this small village.

⑦ Turn left at the lane. Take the bridleway to the right of the drive leading to **The White House**. Look out for the nicely carved stone by the signpost. Stay on the bridleway beyond the house as it becomes stony and messy underfoot. On reaching a second property, pass to the left of this and proceed forward along the track. The bridleway soon has a tarmac surface. On reaching a 'staggered' crossroads turn left to the **Little Mill Inn**. (¹/₄ mile)

⑧ After lunch, turn right along the lane from the pub. Have a look at the large waterwheel on the right, though, before you proceed. Stay on the lane as it swings round to the left. About 400 yards later it forks – take the right fork, ignoring the one to the left for **Long Lee**. At **Laneside Farm** keep forward up the stony sunken lane – be prepared to

step aside if you hear oncoming horses or vehicles. After some distance the view opens out. The old road starts to level out and once again **Lantern Pike** is the highest piece of ground ahead. The track swings right and starts to rise. Ignore another track coming in from the left. Nearly ¹/₂ mile later, ignore a track heading downhill sharp right. (1¹/₄ miles)

⑨ Continue for 250 yards, then walk straight through the farm known as **Wethercotes**. Keep forward to reach a lane. Take care here. Although it doesn't look like it, vehicles do use it. The view from here is 'interesting'. (¹/₄ mile)

⑩ Turn right for 250 yards, then left on a path opposite a driveway to your right. Keep forward beside a wall on your right. At the wall corner, bear half right downhill, aiming to the right of the property below. The path brings you to a gap-stile. Pass through this and walk beside the fence beyond. Turn right along the drive for a few yards, then left down a cobbled lane. (¹/₄ mile)

⑪ Turn left at the road, **Spinnerbottom**. There are some fascinating houses around this part of **Birch Vale**, particularly **The Crescent** on the left. Cross the **River Sett** and 100 yards later turn left onto the **Sett Valley Trail**. Rise up

THE WELCOMING LITTLE MILL INN, AT ROWARTH

the path beyond before swinging left along the Trail away from the road. **Lantern Pike** will appear more impressive along here when you glimpse it through the trees. (¹/₄ mile)

The Sett Valley Trail is less than 3

miles long and was originally the route of the railway that used to run between New Mills and Hayfield.

⑫ Stay on the Trail all the way back to the car park. (1 mile)

Date walk completed:

Walk 5

AROUND LADYBOWER: FAIRHOLMES TO BAMFORD

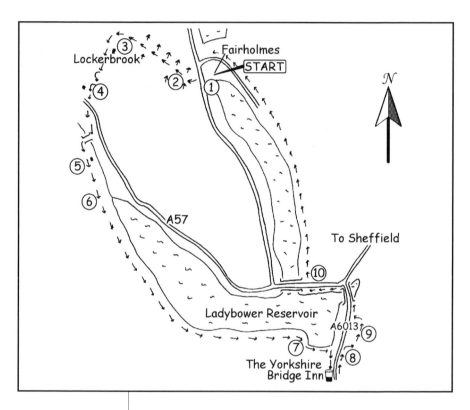

Distance:
9³/₄ miles
(visit the pub after
5¹/₄ miles)
Starting point:
Fairholmes car park.
GR 173893

Map: OS Outdoor Leisure 1 The Peak District – Dark Peak Area

How to get there: *Turn off the A57 Snake Road just west of the point where it is joined by the A6013 at Ladybower. This dead-end road reaches the Fairholmes car park after 2¹/₂ miles.*

LADYBOWER RESERVOIR

*M*uch of this walk runs beside the Ladybower Reservoir in North Derbyshire and the scenery is stunning. This was the area that became famous for, amongst other things, being the place where the Dambusters practised their bombing runs during World War II before tackling the real thing in Germany. That all seems long ago but is very much part of our history. After a climb from the car park at the beginning, this is a relatively easy, flattish walk. The Yorkshire Bridge Inn is another of these excellent pubs that seem to abound around here and will provide an enjoyable lunch, with good views.

The *Famous* **Yorkshire Bridge Inn** – as the sign outside reads – is found on the A6013 north of Bamford and is a super pub. There is plenty of choice, foodwise, so you could go for something plain and simple, such as pot roasted lamb or lamb chops, or a more unusual dish – Chicken Italiano perhaps. You may prefer something lighter and, if so, there are plenty of sandwiches, including hot tuna melt, steak or tuna mayonnaise. There are also vegetarian meals – garlic mushrooms and fresh ricotta and spinach tortellini and so on. Good beers are the order of the day too: Timothy Taylor Landlord, Theakston Old Peculier and Theakston Best Bitter.

Food is served every weekday and Saturday from 12 noon until 2 pm and then from 6 pm until 9 pm (9.30 pm on Friday and Saturday). On a Sunday, a busy day in the Peak District, expect to have food available from 12 noon until 8.30 pm.

Telephone: *01433 651361.*

 *The Walk*

① Leave the car park by the exit for cars. On the opposite side of the road is a Forest Walk signed for **Lockerbrook** and you should follow this. (¹/₄ mile)

② Cross **Locker Brook** itself – it's been straightened here! Take the middle track beyond rising uphill. You reach a haul road. Cross this to the steps opposite and 20 yards later this path swings left uphill and you cross the haul road again. Follow the raised path opposite as it bears left for **Lockerbrook**. This path zig-zags uphill. After passing through a tumbled-down wall the path swings left to pass through a wicket gate into the open.

Lockerbrook is to the left. (¹/₄ mile)

③ Follow the path forward to reach a stony track with a wooden weather station on the right. Turn left along the track. Pass through a gate to walk past **Lockerbook Outdoor Activities Centre**. At the top of the rise the track forks – take the left fork. Just 5 yards later ignore the path on the left, then 40 yards after this ignore a track to the left and a path to the right. Continue to descend. (¹/₂ mile)

④ The stony track brings you to a tarmac lane with **Hagg Farm** to your right. Bear left downhill to the **Snake Road**. Cross to the bridleway opposite and follow this into the valley bottom to go over the **River Ashop**. Bear left along the track beyond it, heading downstream. (¹/₄ mile)

⑤ After climbing uphill for a while from a stone outbuilding, the track swings right. You should fork left along the track beyond the gate. Subsequently ignore a **Peak & Northern Footpaths Society** signpost on the right to descend to a wider track 30 yards later. Bear right along this. The drone of the cars on the other side of the valley is a bit of a pain but this is one of the disadvantages of modern life! (¹/₂ mile)

⑥ Before long the river flows into the reservoir. Half left ahead is the rocky outcrop of **Crook Hill** (1,250 feet). Ignore a number of tracks and paths to the right. **Ashopton Viaduct** should be in view before long. (3 miles)

The villages of Ashopton and Derwent were sacrificed when Ladybower Reservoir was constructed. The villagers all lost their homes, of course. When the water level is low, some of the features of the villages can still be seen.

⑦ On reaching the dam wall turn left along it. At the far side of the

LADYBOWER RESERVOIR WITH WIN HILL ABOVE

35

wall is the overflow, with a stone laid on 25th September 1945 by His Majesty King George VI. Turn right at the road to reach the **Yorkshire Bridge Inn**. (½ mile)

⑧ Return to the dam wall after lunch and cross to the memorial opposite. (¼ mile)

Although it looks like a war memorial, it in fact commemorates the building of the dams. Howden Reservoir was built between 1900 and 1910 and holds 1,980,000,000 gallons and Ladybower 6,300,000,000. The latter was built between 1935 and 1945.

Climb the steps to the right of the memorial and bear left at the top to reach **Heatherdene car park**. You will see that this is the start of the **Derwent Valley Heritage Way**. (½ mile)

The Derwent Valley Heritage Way was opened in 2003 and follows the course of the Derwent for some 55 miles south from where

you stand. It ends at the River Trent. In between it passes through some lovely scenery and highlights a fascinating industrial landscape.

⑨ Walk through the car park and descend to the road. Cross this and turn right to cross the **Ladybower Viaduct**. To the left is the unmistakable summit of **Win Hill**. Turn left along the road on the far side of the viaduct. (¾ mile)

⑩ Immediately *before* **Ashopton Viaduct** turn right and follow the footpath/tarmac lane heading uphill away from the road. When this swings right keep forward through the gate along the public bridleway. This will take you all the way back to the car park. As you proceed, ignore all footpaths to the right, including the one leading uphill signposted '**Slippery Stones**'. The lane you're on descends towards the wall of **Derwent Reservoir**. Swing left in front of this before bearing left on a path back to the car park itself. (3 miles)

Date walk completed:

Walk 6

MAM NICK, BRADWELL AND CASTLETON

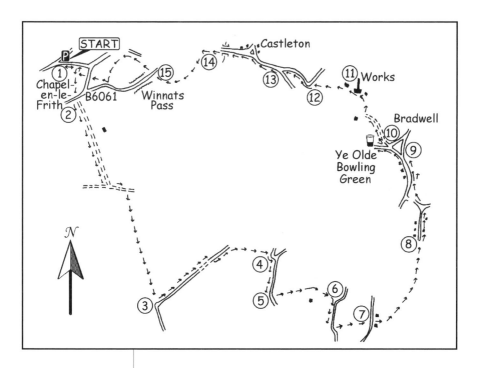

Distance:
10½ miles
(visit the pub
after 6½ miles)

Starting point:
Mam Nick car park
(pay and display).
GR 123832

Map: OS Outdoor Leisure 1 The Peak District – Dark Peak Area
(and a tiny bit of Outdoor Leisure 24 The Peak District – White
Peak Area)

How to get there: From Sparrowpit, east of
Chapel-en-le-Frith, take the B6061 north-eastwards towards
Castleton. Just over 2¾ miles later ignore the right fork
to Castleton. Keep left then for about ½ mile. The car park
is in the angle of the road you're on and the road turning
sharp right for Mam Tor and Edale.

LOOKING BACK TOWARDS MAM TOR FROM THE SOUTH

*T*his is an unusual route heading in the opposite direction from the one most walkers will be following! I'm sure you'll enjoy it but it is a bit different. From the car park below Mam Tor, tracks lead you south to Batham Gate, a Roman road, and then east with much evidence of quarrying, to eventually go northwards, linking Bradwell with Castleton. The circuit gives you a chance to see what man has done to the landscape in the past and what he's still doing to it today. There's what could be described as a 'sting in the tail', too – see what you think.

Ye Olde Bowling Green in Bradwell is open 'all day', which means that if you're there from 12 noon any day of the week you should be able to get something to eat and drink. It's an interesting pub with friendly staff. The beers are Timothy Taylor Landlord, Adnams Bitter (a personal favourite) and Stones Bitter. There may also be a guest such as Black Sheep Bitter.

There's a carvery on a Sunday and an interesting menu every day. Bowling Green lamb hotpot sounds tasty and so does Chef's Chilli Con Carne, though whether you should be eating this with 4 miles still to walk I'll leave up to you! If you do fancy something lighter, then there are sandwiches and jacket potatoes, too.

Telephone: *01433 620450.*

 *The Walk*

① Leave the car park and turn left along the road for 300 yards to a bridlegate on your right. Go through and follow the stony path towards an old disused quarry. Keep to the right of it. The track beyond takes you away from **Mam Tor**. You reach a road. (¹/₂ mile)

'Mam Tor', perhaps not surprisingly if you think about it, means 'Mother Hill'. It obviously had great significance for ancient man who built a hillfort on it. It should be possible to see the hillfort from a number of points on the walk, depending on the light.

② Cross to the metal gate opposite and follow the tarmac drive beyond. Where the driveway turns left towards the farm, continue forward on the stony track for ¹/₂ mile. Turn left at a T-junction of tracks. After 200 yards pass through a gate and then another immediately on your right. Do not follow the **Limestone Way** alongside the wall on your right – instead walk along the track by the fence on your left. At the end of the field, continue forward between two fences running roughly parallel to each other. After 300 yards enter another field and proceed along the track for ³/₄ mile to reach **Batham Gate**, a Roman road no less. (2¹/₄ miles)

③ Turn left here and continue for nearly a mile, passing through the workings of **Moss Rake**. Just beyond **Moss Rake** (and 70 yards after the road runs between walls again) cross the stile on your right. Walk alongside the wall on your left, with the road the other side, for 450 yards. Pass through a wall in front and bear slightly right down into the dry dale knows as **Green Dale**. At the far end of the valley, pass through the small gate onto the road. Turn right. (1¹/₄ miles)

④ Pass the entrance to **Moss Rake Quarry** and rise up to a T-junction. Turn right for **Little Hucklow**. (¹/₄ mile)

⑤ About 500 yards later, just before a left-hand bend, climb the step-over by a gate on the left and follow the track down into the woodland of **Earl Rake**. Climb a step-stile, continuing on the track downhill. With a farm to your right the track becomes a path. Within 100 yards you reach a hollow and there, beneath a large beech tree, climb the simple step-over on your right. *This is easy to miss so take care!* Follow the path down the right side of **Jennings Dale**. The (sometimes overgrown) path brings you to a lane. (1/2 mile)

⑥ Turn right here for 200 yards. Turn left down the walled path –

technically a road. This is another **Green Dale**! (1/2 mile)

⑦ Cross the main road carefully and follow the path to the left of the gable end opposite. Look to your left, though, to get a glimpse of 16th century **Hazlebadge Hall**. On reaching a field, walk forward for 10 yards, cross a track, then bear half left, ascending it. Aim for the highest part of the field but as you near it steer to the right of the flat raised area (but to the left of a small quarry). Follow the vague grassy track through the remains of a gateway in a tumbled-down wall. Head for the nearest houses of **Bradwell** on the grass track/path.

YE OLDE BOWLING GREEN, BRADWELL

Pass through a stile to the left of a gate. ($^1/_2$ mile)

⑧ Walk straight down the road beyond, ignoring all lanes off it, and 200 yards later where the road opens out, '**The Green**', bear left downhill for 30 yards. Descend the steps beyond three stone 'posts'. Keep forward along the pavement, beside the cottages on your right, to reach the road. Proceed along the road through **Bradwell**. ($^1/_2$ mile)

As you go, look out for a small plaque on a cottage on the left-hand side of the road opposite the church. Samuel Fox, the inventor of the folding umbrella, was born here.

⑨ After 500 yards fork left along **Town Lane**, keeping the playing fields to your right. At the crossroads, turn left up **Smalldale**. Stay on this and, ignoring the road forking left, you reach **Ye Olde Bowling Green** on the right. ($^1/_4$ mile)

⑩ After lunch return to the crossroads. Turn left at **Corner Cottage**. Walk along the lane beyond, passing the pub to your left. This is a tarmac path initially before changing to a stony surface. It bends left before passing through a gateway towards a property 60 yards ahead. You should turn right *before* the gateway along a walled tarmac path. Where the path forks 60 yards later keep forward along the tarmac path, descending fairly quickly after a few yards. This brings you to the cement works. ($^3/_4$ mile)

⑪ With the cement works on your right cross the access road, proceeding on the stony bridleway beside a fence. Where another track comes in from the left bear right beside a hedge. Pass under a gantry. On joining another track on the left bear right along it. Pass under another gantry and bear left uphill for a few yards before taking the fenced bridleway to your right. There's a tall chimney to your right. Before long the works are out of sight, though not out of earshot. ($^1/_4$ mile)

⑫ With **Pindle Cottage** (1854) on your right, proceed straight forward to the lane. Turn left along this, following the right-hand bend uphill. Views of the **Dark Peak** are soon to be enjoyed – **Win Hill** to the right and the rounded top of **Lose Hill** to the left of it. Stay on the lane. ($^1/_2$ mile)

⑬ When another lane joins from the left, bear right towards **Castleton**. A marvellous view of **Mam Tor** lies ahead as you descend into the village. Ignore the entrance to **Cave Dale** on your left to enter **Bargate**. Descend to a grass triangle, keeping to the left of it.

Continue along the level lane to the left of the **Youth Hostel**. Stay on this until you reach some shops, with a stream beyond. Cross the stone bridge over the stream and head forward uphill, ignoring the left turn to **Peak Cavern**, to climb **Goosehill**. Where it forks, take the right fork uphill. This soon becomes a wide stony path taking you into the countryside. (¹/₂ mile)

Castleton is famous for a number of things – its caverns (including The Devil's Arse), Peveril Castle and, of course, Blue John. The name is supposed to come from the French 'bleu jaune' meaning 'blue yellow' because these are two of the colours in this unusual mineral. It seems as though the seams of Blue John are not endless and so, if you have any, its value may rise in the future.

⑭ Walk along the bottom side of two fields to reach the lane, with **Speedwell Cavern** to your left and **Winnats Pass** beyond. (¹/₂ mile)

⑮ Cross the road and take the step-over to follow the path for **Treak**

Cliff Cavern. Cross another path after 30 yards. Pass through a gate and walk on the top side of some trees. Bear left up the 'made-up' path to reach **Treak Cliff**. Keep left of the entrance, following the public footpath on the top side of the cavern buildings. This rises uphill, swinging round to the left to a wicket gate. Ignore the step-over here, pass through the gate and head forward on quite a long ascending traverse to reach the **Blue John Cavern**. Cross the yard in front of it, passing through a gate on the far side. The path beyond rises and swings steadily left until you are walking alongside some marshy ground to your right. As the ground levels out, head for the gable end of a building ahead. Turn right when you reach the wall. Walk alongside it to a gate. Pass through this and head across the field to another. Cross the road and fork right across the first field to another gate. On the road beyond, turn left back to **Mam Nick car park**. (1¹/₂ miles)

Date walk completed:

REDMIRES RESERVOIRS, LONGSHAW AND RINGINGLOW

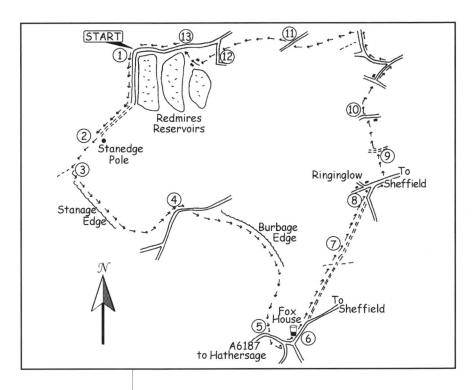

Distance:
12³/₄ miles
(pub stop after
5³/₄ miles)

Starting point:
The car park at
Redmires Upper
Reservoir.
GR 256856

Map: OS Outdoor Leisure 1 The Peak District – Dark Peak Area

How to get there: *Follow Ringinglow Road westward
from Sheffield. At Ringinglow take the right turn. After that
keep left at each road junction to reach the car park beside
the most westerly of the three reservoirs at Redmires. It's
on the right just before a left-hand bend.*

LOOKING NORTH-WESTWARDS ON STANAGE EDGE

*T*he names of some of the places you pass on this route are truly enticing. Surely Stanedge Pole, Carl Wark, Fox House, Houndkirk Moor, Lady Canning's Plantation, Redmires Conduit make you want to get out and try this route, the longest in the book? It won't let you down. When you're walking across Houndkirk Moor you will be surprised to see Sheffield nestling over there to your right. Do it on a misty day, though, and it will be as if you're miles away from anywhere. The Fox House is an excellent place to stop albeit just under the halfway point.

The **Fox House** at Longshaw is a pub I had never visited until the day I first walked this route, and I wish I had discovered it years ago. It's friendly, welcoming, and full of interesting photographs of the area – a visit to the loo is worthwhile just to look at the pictures on the way.

Food is served from 12 noon until 10 pm – and what food! The main courses include dishes like pork, apple and Somerset cider sausages, beef, mushroom and ale pie, or chilled Cajun salmon salad. Even the sandwiches aren't run of the mill, with oak smoked Cheddar and fruit chutney or bacon and Cheddar melt fillings to choose from, amongst others. The beers are Black Sheep Bitter, Bass, Stones and Tetleys.

▌ **Telephone:** *01433 630374.*

The Walk

① Turn right out of the car park, with the reservoir to your left. About 600 yards later, turn right up the gravel byway. This rises steadily to **Stanedge Pole** 2/3 mile later. At 1,437 feet (or thereabouts) this would have been a marker for travellers in centuries long gone though it appears that the existing pole itself isn't the original one. (1 mile)

② Continue along the track to the right of the pole and 600 yards later, where the track bears right, bear left towards a wall 60 yards ahead. The view ahead widens out. **Win Hill** is the most obvious feature ahead with **Lose Hill** beyond it. **Mam Tor** is to the right of the **Hope Cement Works**, the building with the tall chimney. Keep to the right of the wall. Turn left beyond it so that you're walking with the wall on your left and the southern end of **Stanage Edge** on your right and yes it *is* 'Stanage' not 'Stanedge' – though they're all pronounced

'Stannij'. **Hathersage** is down to your right and its church spire may be visible. (1/2 mile)

③ When the wall on your left ends, stay on the path in front with the Edge to your right. Rise up to the rocks ahead and proceed towards the trig point. The path keeps to the left of this though – aim for **Burbage Edge** over 1/2 mile ahead. Initially the path descends fairly steeply then it levels out across the moor. Look out for a stone laid in the path to the memory of Martin Davies '1959-1995 A Walker'. (1 3/4 miles)

④ On reaching the road turn left and cross two bridges at **Upper Burbage Bridge**. Just beyond the second bridge pass through the first gate on your right and follow the path as it bears gently left. The stony track descends steadily and, with **Burbage Edge** above to your left, you follow this for over 1 1/2 miles. As you go you'll see climbers on your left, and on your right the two flat-topped outcrops of **Higger Tor** and **Carl Wark**, the latter, lower than the former, is an ancient hillfort. Ignore the **Sheffield Country Walk** that crosses the path you're on. Yes, rather surprisingly you're in the City of Sheffield. You reach the road via a small car park. (2 miles)

⑤ Cross the A6187 into the National Trust's **Longshaw Estate**. Head forward under the pine trees, bearing left to reach the main path after 100 yards. Bear left along this to the road. Turn left here before turning right at the junction to reach the **Fox House**. (¹/₂ mile)

The Fox House seems to have nothing to do with foxes.

Tradition has it that it was built in the 18th century for a man called Fox who lived nearby at Highlow.

⑥ After lunch turn left out of the **Fox House** and follow the main road gently uphill towards **Sheffield**. On a gentle right-hand bend 500 yards later, bear left along the public byway. This is **Houndkirk Road** – a marvellously evocative name – across **Houndkirk Moor** and you will be on it for over 2 miles. Cross the driveway to **Parson House Outdoor Pursuit Centre** and rise steadily uphill. A footpath crosses the byway. The rocky outcrop ¹/₂ mile to the right is **Houndkirk**

THE FOX HOUSE, LONGSHAW

Hill and there are interesting views of **Sheffield** to your right as you proceed. To the left you see the **Ox Stones** with a trig point to their right. (1 3/4 miles)

According to an old book of 'Rambles' that I own, written by Chas H. Chandler and printed in 1913 (it cost ninepence by the way), Houndkirk Road was the 'old coach road which formerly linked Sheffield to Buxton'. There is something particularly satisfying to be following in the footsteps of Mr Chandler some 90 years later.

⑦ Just beyond a kink in the byway look out for a guidepost on your left showing the distance to **Tideswell** and **Buxton**.

Chas H. Chandler wrote at this point: '... there is an old milestone showing 10 miles to Tideswell and 17 to Buxton.'

Some 300 yards later another byway crosses **Houndkirk Road**. Ignore it. Eventually you walk alongside **Lady Canning's Plantation** on your left. (1 mile)

⑧ You leave **Houndkirk Road** when you reach a tarmac road. Bear left along the road into **Ringinglow**, noting the unusual tollhouse on the left. Turn right at the main road for 175 yards. Turn left along the first footpath on your left, walking down

the left side of two fields before crossing a narrow field. After this, head down into the valley, aiming for the bottom right-hand corner of the field. (3/4 mile)

⑨ At **Clough Lane** turn left before 25 yards later passing through a stile on the right. Go over another stile on your left 5 yards later, crossing the field ahead to enter the trees. Cross a footbridge beneath the trees and rise up out of the trees to go over a field. Cross a stile and proceed along the right side of the field beyond to reach a lane by a farm. It's hard to believe that Sheffield City Centre is just a few miles away. (1/4 mile)

⑩ Turn left up the lane. After 25 yards, take the footpath on the right. Walk on the left side of the field for 200 yards, descend some steps and walk alongside a stream on your left. Cross a footbridge and proceed past some cottages on your left, continuing along the drive to a lane. Keep forward here, along **David Lane**. Pass the **Hole in the Wall**, on your right, as you go. At the T-junction turn left, noting a small seat within a few yards. Stay on the lane as it bears sharply right, passing **Fulwood Hall**. Turn right along another lane immediately beyond **Bole Hill Farm**. Pass **Moorside** on the right. Ignore a path to left and right at the brow of the hill. Descend for 125 yards before turning left alongside **Redmires Conduit**. This 19th-century watercourse isn't always visible but you'll be walking beside it for some way. (1¼ miles)

⑪ Cross a lane, continuing opposite on the path beside the conduit. Stay on this path to another lane. (1 mile)

⑫ Cross this and follow a concessionary path between low walls, entering the wood beyond by a step-stile. The conduit is quite clear in this wood, at least initially. Climb a wall before bearing right downhill beside it. Cross another conduit. A few yards later turn right along the road rising uphill between houses. Just beyond them turn left on the roadway, passing various inspection chambers. In front of the gate turn right along the path into the trees. Stay on this to reach a roadway. (½ mile)

⑬ Turn left, with **Redmires Middle Reservoir** on your left (though not visible). Pass what appears to be a roadside memorial, with three fishes carved in the stonework, dated 1828.

It seems that what appears to be a memorial is in fact a stone from a pub that used to stand hereabouts – the Grouse and Trout. Chas H. Chandler mentioned in passing that the pub was painted pink in 1913. It would presumably have been demolished like so many properties that were near to reservoirs in those days.

You then reach the **Upper Reservoir**, from where you return to your car. (½ mile)

Date walk completed:

48

BOLLINGTON, WHITE NANCY AND RAINOW

BRIDGE 29 ON THE MACCLESFIELD CANAL, SOUTH OF BOLLINGTON

Distance:
11 miles
(reach the pub
after 6¹/₄ miles)
Starting point:
Adlington Road
Ranger Centre.
GR 931781

Map: OS Explorer 268 Wilmslow, Macclesfield & Congleton

How to get there: *Bollington is on the B5091 north-east
of Macclesfield. Approaching on the A523, turn off
eastwards at the roundabout to the south of Prestbury. Just
over 1¹/₂ miles later turn left into Adlington Road. The car
park is down here on the left.*

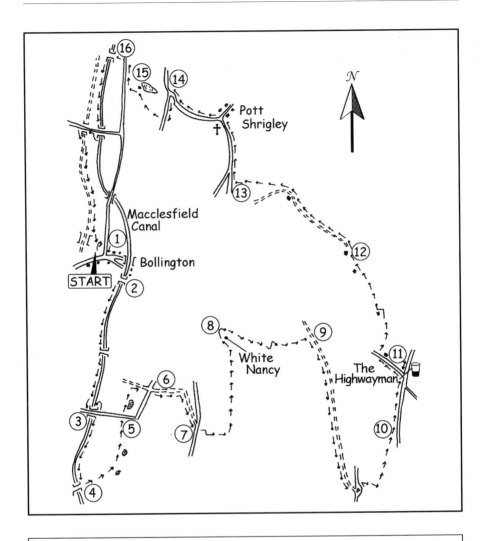

*T*his is a slightly overlooked part of the Peak District perhaps, but it shouldn't be. The Saddle of Kerridge gives fine views across the Cheshire Plain and it's really enjoyable walking beside the Macclesfield Canal and along the Middlewood Way. You'll get the chance to visit White Nancy and how many times have you driven past and looked up at it and wondered what it was?

Perched on the hillside overlooking Greater Manchester, the **Highwayman**, near Rainow, is one of those pubs it's a pleasure to find. It's named after one of two legendary highwaymen who used to frequent these parts – Tom King and Charles Pym.

The food is good quality and there's ample choice. I tried the Chicken Burrito with chips and salad garnish, sour cream and salsa and enjoyed it but there's much more, such as salads (ham and beef for example), open sandwiches, Cumberland sausage, scampi and black pudding with mushrooms and onions. Thwaites beers are for sale – Thoroughbred, Bitter and Lancaster Bomber.

The pub is open from 12 noon until 3 pm on Monday, Tuesday and Wednesday, and all day on Thursday, Friday, Saturday and Sunday. Food is served from 12 noon until 2.30 pm on Monday to Saturday (and 5 pm to 9 pm on Thursday to Saturday) and on Sunday from 12 noon until 2.30 pm and 5 pm until 8 pm.

Telephone: *01625 573245.*

① From the car park turn right up **Adlington Road**. At the main road turn left and 100 yards later fork right up **Hurst Lane**. When the road bends sharp right keep forward onto the **Macclesfield Canal**. Turn right. (¹/₄ mile)

The Macclesfield Canal is just over 25 miles long and links the Trent & Mersey Canal with the Peak Forest Canal.

② Pass under **bridge 27**. This is an interesting stretch of canalside walking, passing through the houses. Pass **Bollington Wharf** and a large mill before going under **bridge 28**.

The countryside beckons with **Kerridge Hill** to your left. (1 mile)

③ **Bridge 29** is interesting. Walk up the right side, keep left and you'll find yourself on the other side of the canal! It will make more sense when you do it. A lovely stretch of canal beneath the trees awaits you. (¹/₄ mile)

④ Leave the canal at **bridge 30**, rising to the left of it to the stile. Proceed along the track away from the canal. Pass a pond on your left. At the pond on your right, cross the stile opposite. With your back to this, head half right to a gate. Cross the stile by this gate. Walk alongside a third pond on your right. Pass through a squeezer at the end of it.

Follow the hedge/fence on your left to a road. (½ mile)

⑤ Cross this, pass through a kissing gate and head for a second gate 30 yards away. Proceed beside a hedge on your right, with another pond beyond. Ignore a slab bridge on your right to pass through a squeeze-stile ahead. Keep along the right side of the field beyond. On reaching a gravel track, turn right. (½ mile)

⑥ At the road, walk up the track opposite. Keep in the same direction, passing through the gateway of **Endon House**. Bear right immediately beyond it, passing **Endon Cottage** on your left. About 70 yards later ignore a lower, level, track. Rise up to the road. (½ mile)

⑦ Cross this, aiming for **Endon Quarry**. Within 50 yards, turn right on a path which swings left. Climb uphill passing a property on your right. Proceed to the crest of the hill. Turn left here, ignoring a stile in the wall. Walk along the **Saddle of Kerridge** between the fence and the wall. After a while you need to walk on the other side of the wall, though still along the ridge. Eventually, you swing back to the other side of the wall to reach **White Nancy** at the far end. (1 mile)

White Nancy is an unusual

feature, prominent from the area below the Saddle of Kerridge. It seems like so many things now to suffer at the hand of vandals who presumably take great delight in covering it with graffiti which is then painted over, ready for the next assault. It appears to be either a memorial to the Battle of Waterloo or to a deceased daughter of the man who had it built.

⑧ Descend the pitched path beyond this unusual feature. You're only ¾ mile from where you started – and they say walking is futile. At a tarmac track, 200 yards later, turn right. Stay on this, passing a cattle grid. Ahead, half left is **Savio House** which you'll pass shortly. Where the track forks, take the fork descending to the left. Stay on this past another cattle grid. Shortly afterwards, at another track, turn left towards an old mill. Before reaching it, turn sharp right through a stile. Cross the bridge beyond. Head forward before swinging left and uphill on a clear path. Follow some steps along the left side of a field. Continue with the wall on your left and **Savio House** beyond. On reaching a stile (where you can turn left or right), keep forward, bearing slightly right towards the hilltop ahead. This brings you to the Peak Park boundary, **Oakenbank Lane**. (¾ mile)

⑨ Turn right for ½ mile. **Rainow** is

ahead to the right. At the grass triangle turn left and left again. Some 50 yards later, with **Lower House** on your left, climb the stile on the right. Cross the field to the stile to the left of a holly tree. Keep alongside the wall on your right passing an outbuilding on your left. Cross a step-stile, noting the stile uphill to your left. To get to it walk forward 50 yards then turn left uphill. Walk up the left side of the field beyond. Keep in the same direction across the one after. Bear slightly left across the next one to

climb a step-stile. Proceed across the rougher ground to another step-stile. Then walk up the left side of the subsequent field to pass through a gate. From here aim just left of the gate at the top of the field ahead. Cross the corner of the field after to reach the road. (1¼ miles)

⑩ Turn left, taking care. Cross onto the right side of the road *as soon as possible*. Keep forward at the staggered crossroads to reach the **Highwayman**. (¼ mile)

THE HIGHWAYMAN, NEAR RAINOW

53

⑪ Return to the crossroads and turn right for **Bollington** and 500 yards later pass **Billinge Head Farm** on your right. After 80 yards turn right along a track. Pass through a gate. Fork right on the descending track and 400 yards later, immediately beyond a property on your left, cross a stile. Bear right down the field for a stile 30 yards from the far right corner. Proceed down the right side of the field beyond. Where the hedge ends aim just to the right of the farmhouse ahead. Cross the step-stile in front of this. Descend into the yard and bear half right through a gate. Descend the path beyond. Cross a slab-bridge and another just beyond. Bear right to a stile at the right end of the wall ahead. Then head up the driveway leading away from the house to your left. (1 mile)

⑫ Stay on this for 1/2 mile. At **Berristall Hall** (1881) keep on the driveway for 100 yards. As the drive leaves the wall on your right walk forward *alongside* the wall. Keep this on your right as you head towards the trig point on **Nab Head**. Cross a couple of stiles either side of the parking area and walk forward past another property to descend some awkward steps and reach **Spuley Lane**. (1 mile)

⑬ Turn right and 200 yards later keep forward at the road junction into **Pott Shrigley**. Try and get on the right side of the road before the church. Follow the main road round to the left. Walk beside it for 1/2 mile. (3/4 mile)

⑭ Turn left along **Long Lane**. Pass the old quarry entrance, then 80 yards past the **Nab Farm** entrance, take the footpath on your right (for **Sugar Lane**). After 50 yards fork right as the path splits. Keep forward with an old quarry on your right to reach a wall. Keep this beside you (on your left). Subsequently keep left to follow the path between two walls. This becomes a sunken lane beneath holly trees. It can be quite overgrown. On reaching a driveway, keep forward. (1/2 mile)

⑮ At **Pool Cottage** turn left, though **Styperson Pool** is worth a glance to your right. At **Sugar Lane** turn right for 200 yards. Turn left immediately beyond **Queens Gate House**. (1/4 mile)

⑯ Cross **bridge 22** over the canal. Turn right and keep right (passing under the bridge) to walk alongside the **Macclesfield Canal** again. After 1/2 mile, immediately beyond **bridge 25**, turn right up the steps to a lane. Turn left and cross a roadbridge. Turn left beyond this to reach the **Middlewood Way**.

The Middlewood Way is yet another old railway line that has

WHITE NANCY

been put to good use recently by being re-created as a trail for walkers and horse-riders etc. It runs for 11 miles between Macclesfield and Marple. In many places it is very near to the Macclesfield Canal, as will be seen from this walk.

Turn right along it but cross it almost immediately, climbing some steps leading up to a path running on the left-hand side of the Way. This is higher than the route you've just crossed. **White Nancy** should be visible ahead. Cross a driveway, continuing on the higher path. With a property on your left, descend some steps to take you to the lower level path. Within 100 yards descend the left side of the route to return to the start. You may wish to keep forward to have a look at the view from the viaduct. (1¼ miles)

Date walk completed:

Walk 9

ERRWOOD RESERVOIR, MACCLESFIELD FOREST AND SHINING TOR

THE CAT & FIDDLE, NEAR BUXTON

Distance:
11¼ miles
(5½ miles to
the pub)

Starting point:
Goyts Lane car park
at the Errwood
Reservoir.
GR 025752

Map: OS Outdoor Leisure 24 The Peak District – White Peak Area

How to get there: From the A5004 north-west of
Buxton, turn off westwards at the 'Goyt Valley' sign
1½ miles out of town. Half a mile later park on the left
just before the small reservoir.

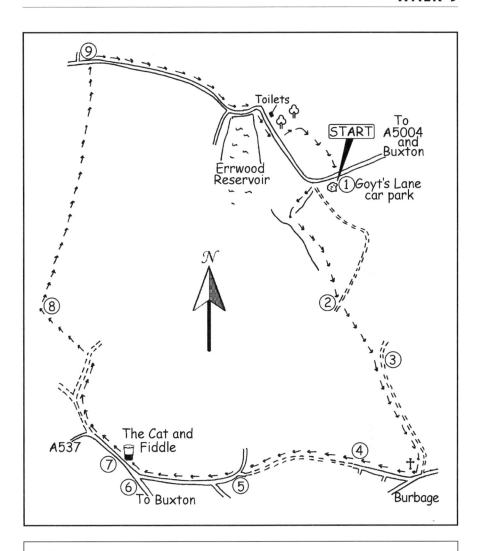

*T*his is a challenging and adventurous walk, with wide-ranging views, taking you from the edge of Errwood Reservoir cross-country to Burbage and then to the very high Cat & Fiddle. The route returns to the reservoir by way of Shining Tor and the marvellous viewpoint of Pym Chair. Although there is some lane and road walking, the panoramas you get will more than make up for it.

Now I'd better get this right. The landlord of the **Cat & Fiddle** says that his pub is 'the highest originally fully licensed pub in England'. So there you have it. It's high! It's popular too with people dropping in on the drive between Macclesfield and Buxton. This will be one of the first roads to close in and around Derbyshire when it snows – though, as we know, we don't get winters like we used to when I were a lad. The pub is in Cheshire these days and its postal address is Macclesfield Forest, which is a rather vague area somewhere west of Buxton.

The Cat & Fiddle opens every day from 11 am and it never shuts before 6 pm (except on Monday, when it closes at 5 pm). It's very much a daytime pub – so they may close in the evening if it's quiet or miserable or foggy etc. If you want to keep your boots on, go into the bar nearest you as you walk up the road. Take them off if you want to go into the lounge and/or dining room.

Everything from sandwiches to steaks is served and the menu is tempting, with dishes such as half a roast chicken, beef chilli with rice and chips, cauliflower bake and chicken, mushroom and bacon pie. Food is available at lunchtime from 11 am each day and is served until 4 pm on Monday and into the early evening on the other days, whenever the pub is open. The beer is Robinson's, so you have the choice of Old Stockport Bitter and various seasonal brews.

Telephone: *01298 23364.*

The Walk

① From the car park entrance, turn left along the lane. At the end of the small reservoir, pass through a gate on the left. The dismantled railway line stretches away to your left. Take the footpath directly ahead signed '**Wildmoorstone Brook**'. This descends quite steeply, with a stream on your left in a fairly deep cleft in the hillside. About 400 yards later, with another stream ahead, follow a minor path on the left to a signpost. At the signpost, take the path heading left, signed '**Burbage**'. This heads up a gentle valley with the brook to your right. Cross some duckboarding and a bridge – all the time keeping the brook on your right. Beyond another footbridge the path gets steeper and you ascend to reach the old railway line. On the right is the blocked tunnel where the railway would have come through the hillside from Burbage. (1 mile)

The Cromford and High Peak Railway used to run all the way from Whaley Bridge to the High Peak Junction on the Cromford Canal. This was to be a link from one canal (Cromford) to another (the Peak Forest). It has been closed for some years though a stretch of it has become a popular walking route – the High Peak Trail – between Cromford and Dowlow. There is talk at this time of the Trail being extended further north towards Whaley Bridge.

② Walk right towards the tunnel for 10 yards. Turn left on the path for 'Buxton' and 'Bishop's Lane'. This rises up the right side of a wall for 375 yards. On reaching the wall-corner keep forward (bearing slightly right) towards the brow of the hill. Keep forward, ignoring a lesser path to the right. Almost immediately, descend fairly steadily towards the right-hand end of a line of trees 100 yards ahead. Cross the stile and descend diagonally right. **Buxton** stretches out ahead. (1/2 mile)

③ On reaching a tarmac lane turn right, passing the properties at **Edgemoor** as well as an attractive garden. Keep forward past **Plex Lodge** to your left. You're walking along **Bishop's Lane**. Stay on this for another 1/2 mile. Fork right into

TRIG POINT AT SHINING TOR

Nursery Lane. Turn right again at the main road, then 130 yards later (past the church on your right) fork right onto **Macclesfield Old Road**. Stay on this road for just under $^1/_2$ mile until you reach **Level Lane** to your left – ignore this. (1$^1/_4$ miles)

④ Keep forward uphill though the road now starts to deteriorate, becoming a stony track rising into open countryside. You pass over a dismantled railway line – the same one that went through the tunnel that you saw on the other side of the hill earlier. **Solomon's Temple** is visible on **Grin Low** to your left. Ignore a number of paths to left and right. The track rises until you get a view of the **Cat & Fiddle** ahead to the right. Follow this stony track for about a mile. (1$^1/_2$ miles)

MILESTONE NEAR THE CAT & FIDDLE

⑤ Descend to **Derbyshire Bridge**, so called because it used to be on the boundary between Cheshire and Derbyshire. The road to the right cannot be entered by vehicles. Keep forward along the lane that takes you up to the A537 a mile away – ignore a road to the left as you go. This is a rather tedious climb but it will be worthwhile later. (1 mile)

⑥ Turn right at the main road to reach the **Cat & Fiddle** itself. ($^1/_4$ mile)

⑦ After lunch turn right along the

road and 300 yards later, on a left-hand bend, keep forward on the track. **Shutlingsloe** is away to your left. Another 300 yards later bear right along another track. Stay on this, with a farm down to your left. Ignore a stile to the right (for **Goytsclough Quarry**) just before a kissing gate. Proceed through the kissing gate and 200 yards later turn left through another kissing gate, signed '**Shining Tor**'. Walk along the clear path beside the wall for $^1/_2$ mile. (1$^1/_2$ miles)

⑧ On reaching the wall (with the

trig point on the other side), turn right along the path, with the wall on your left. This path has some 'give' in it so don't think you're suffering the after effects of that beer you had earlier – it was constructed using a special material that gives it that extra bounce, disconcerting though it is. You are aiming for **Pym Chair**, the rounded hill straight ahead. After quite a bit of bog-trotting the path becomes grassier. Keep on beside the wall on your left. (2 miles)

Pym Chair is supposed to be named after the highwayman Charles Pym. You can imagine what a good viewpoint this ridge would be for Pym to espy travellers who would subsequently be invited to part with their money.

⑨ Beyond **Pym Chair**, you reach a road. Turn right. As you descend, you'll see there's a grassy path after some distance on the left side of the lane. Keep on down the lane (or the path) until you pass a large car park on the right near the bottom of the hill. Then the road forks. Take the

fork sharp left, with **Errwood Reservoir** beyond. Cross the reservoir wall. Stay on the road as it bears left, then right, passing a toilet block on the left. There are two options here. The route shown on the map is as follows: 350 yards or so beyond the toilet block pass through a wicket gate on your left (immediately beyond a small wood). Follow the path away from the road. This path soon begins to rise before swinging right. With the main road away to your left, pass through an old gateway in a wall. You should then rise steadily to reach the lane you drove along to reach the car park. Turn right to the car park itself.

The other option, if you wish to avoid the path, is to proceed uphill from the toilet block on the road, this steep, straight gradient taking you all the way back to the car park. (2¼ miles)

This testing stretch of road used to be the original route of the Cromford and High Peak Railway line.

Date walk completed:

WYE DALE, CHEE DALE, TADDINGTON AND DEEP DALE

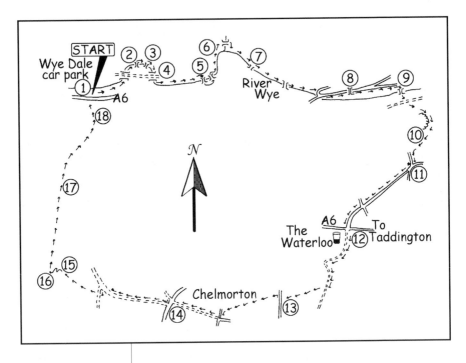

Distance:
9¼ miles
(5¼ miles to
the Waterloo)

Starting point:
Wye Dale car park.
GR 104725

Map: OS Outdoor Leisure 24 The Peak District – White Peak Area

How to get there: *Approaching from the east, drive towards Buxton on the A6, passing the Waterloo which lies to the west of Taddington. Two miles later, at the bottom of the hill, turn right into the car park. Approaching from Buxton, travel east along the A6. After 3 miles or so (just after passing under a bridge) the Wye Dale car park will be on your left.*

THE STEPPING STONES IN CHEE DALE

*Y*ou want adventure? Well, you've got it on this walk. A notice partway along the route describes the path through Chee Dale as 'difficult' and 'likely to flood in wet weather'. It's true too. If it's been wet and the river is up, you will either have to turn back or paddle in the river – you have been warned. Having said that, Chee Dale is well, well worth exploring but you have to be prepared to turn back if the river is high. The rest of the walk is interesting too, taking you along the Monsal Trail into Miller's Dale before lunch near Taddington. Later the Midshires Way takes you into Deep Dale, where the flowers in spring and summer are amazing.

A friendly and popular hostelry beside the A6 just outside Taddington, the **Waterloo** also sits alongside the Limestone Way, which runs up the side of it. In this pub you can keep your boots on, though you may prefer to take 'em off if they're muddy.

Robinson's Best Bitter, Three Shires Mild and Young Tom are for sale. As regards the bar menu there's a good choice, including breaded plaice, home-made steak pie, large baguettes served with various fillings and Roast of the Day with Yorkshire pudding, roast potatoes, fresh veg and gravy.

The Waterloo opens at 12 noon and closes at 11 pm (except Sundays when it closes at 10.30 pm). Food is served from 12 noon until 9 pm on Monday to Saturday and until 6 pm on Sunday.

Telephone: *01298 85230.*

 *The Walk*

① Walk to the bottom end of the car park away from the A6. Follow the bridleway for the **Monsal Trail**. You walk beside the **River Wye** for some distance. After ¹/₂ mile ignore the signs on the right for the Trail and stay by the river to reach **Blackwell Cottages**. (³/₄ mile)

② Cross the footbridge over the river, but note the warning on the bridge about flooding in wet weather. Turn right beyond the bridge, along the riverside path. When the path subsequently forks, take the right fork beside the river. It's worth keeping an eye out for fish, as well as what's underfoot, of course. (¹/₄ mile)

③ On reaching a footbridge, turn left immediately you step onto it. This means you're still walking downstream, with the river on your right. The scenery becomes

increasingly impressive but look out for low-lying nettles in summertime. (¹/₄ mile)

④ Pass under a tall stone bridge, with the **Wye** gurgling along beside you. Look out for climbers on the crags on the far side of the watercourse. You reach the first group of stepping stones. Rather unusually, they don't cross the river, but run down the left side of it. Hopefully, they're not flooded. (¹/₂ mile)

⑤ Another footbridge takes you onto the far side of the river to rise up some steps beyond. After a few yards, where the path forks, take the left fork down some steps and cross another footbridge to walk down the left side of the river again. (¹/₄ mile)

⑥ Another run of stepping stones takes you through the river again. Where the path opens out **Chee Tor** is above to your right. By a shady 'pool' you then clamber up about

25 feet of rough rock 'steps'. It's easier (and safer) going up than down! The path then bears round to the left alongside a stream which flows into the river. Cross a small bridge then a stile after a few yards. Take the right fork after a few more yards to walk beside (if not in) the stream, which is now on your right. Cross another small footbridge. Ignore a vague path heading uphill to the left. Negotiate another, shorter, flight of 'steps'. Beyond this, after much slipping and sliding, you come out in the open. Head to the footbridge ahead. (3/4 mile)

⑦ Don't cross the bridge but keep forward in the river valley, signed '**Miller's Dale**'. On the left is the **Wormhill Scrubs Nature Reserve**. Some distance downriver, pass under a high bridge popular with abseilers. Proceed beside the river for nearly 1/2 mile. On reaching a road turn right before turning left a few yards later. (1 mile)

⑧ After a while, as you pass under the old railway bridge, there is no footway for over 200 yards. Please keep on the right in single file. The first property on the left as you enter **Miller's Dale** is the unusual '**1740 House**'. Just beyond this fork right for '**Litton Mill** only'. Almost

WALKING THROUGH BUTTERBUR IN CHEE DALE

65

immediately there's the remains of the **Meal Mill** on the right, complete with seat and interpretation panel. ($^1/_4$ mile)

⑨ A few yards later, fork right again on a path to cross a footbridge over the river. Bear left uphill beyond this to rise up to the **Monsal Trail**. Cross the Trail to enter the **Miller's Dale Quarry Nature Reserve**. Once you come out into the open the path bears left diagonally uphill. This is a 'steady climb' (in other words fairly steep!). There's an excellent view behind. When you reach the quarry bottom bear left uphill on the path beside the metal fence. This carries you up round the edge of the quarry. Stay beside the fence, or what remains of it, to reach a wall at the top. ($^1/_4$ mile)

⑩ Cross a stile and keep forward to another on the opposite side of the field. Go down the right side of the field beyond, with **Taddington** lying ahead of you. Walk down the left side of the next field, though partway down the field switch to the other side of the wall – still heading in the same direction. Cross another stile into the corner of the field and bear slightly right across the next few fields to reach a walled track. Turn left on this to reach **Lydgate Farm**. ($^1/_2$ mile)

⑪ Turn right on the lane before, 50 yards later, turning right again (ignore a left fork downhill). Stay on this lane for almost $^1/_2$ mile to reach a crossroads. Go straight over to follow the **Limestone Way** and 400 yards later you reach the **Waterloo**. Lunch! ($^1/_2$ mile)

The Limestone Way is a long distance route stretching from Castleton all the way down to Rocester in Staffordshire, with a spur off it running down Masson Hill into Matlock. It has recently been suffering from lack of care and consideration but it is hoped to encourage the authorities to maintain and waymark it.

⑫ Take the track immediately to the left of the pub, rising steadily with views getting better as you go. The track zig-zags, then levels out. About $^3/_4$ mile after leaving the pub you reach a point where there are three gateways and the track you're on is crossed by a footpath; turn right on the path. Ahead on your right is **Fivewells Farm**. Keep on the right-hand side of the first three fields after the track. In the fourth field, head a touch right. (1 mile)

⑬ This brings you to a tarmac lane. Turn right for 5 yards then left through a rough field for 500 yards. The field narrows and you're channelled down into **Chelmorton**. Look out for **Illy Willy Water** on the right just before you get into the village. Pass the **Church Inn**.

As you pass the church – one of the highest in the Peak District – look out on the spire for the gilded locust, the symbol of St John the Baptist, which is also the name of the church.

Just before the road to the left, turn right along a track signposted for the **Midshires Way**. After 250 yards ignore the right fork into the farmyard – bear left and follow the track all the way to the road. (1 mile)

⑭ There are two tracks opposite. Take the left one, still following the **Midshires Way**. Stay on this for $1/2$ mile, ignoring a green lane to the left as you go. As the lane you're on bears away to the right, turn sharp left on another walled track before reaching a stile on the right after 60 yards. Cross this to the stile in the wall opposite. Keep in the same direction to climb a third, then a fourth, stile (beyond an electricity pole in the middle of the field). In the fourth field, cut the corner to climb a stile overlooking **Deep Dale**.

⑮ Zig-zag down into the dale. In June there is an impressive selection of flowers, including orchids. ($3/4$ mile)

⑯ In the valley bottom, turn right. For the next mile you stay in **Deep Dale**. It's a path that needs some concentration as it's uneven underfoot. In summer there are nettles lurking low and out of sight ready to catch your ankles if you're wearing shorts. Then there's the quicksand ... well, you wanted adventure. Yes, quicksand, though it may be deep slurry – what a choice! Don't check it out. It's clear where it is – behind fences so stay on the path and there's absolutely no problem.

⑰ There's only one path as you proceed. It rises at one stage slightly and then drops to a lower level at another. Just keep heading along the valley bottom, ignoring a smaller valley to the right (with a path in it) as you go. Eventually you reach the entrance to a quarry. (1 mile)

⑱ Keep forward down the right side of the access road to reach the A6 with the car park opposite. ($1/4$ mile)

Date walk completed:

MACCLESFIELD FOREST, WILDBOARCLOUGH AND THREE SHIRES HEAD

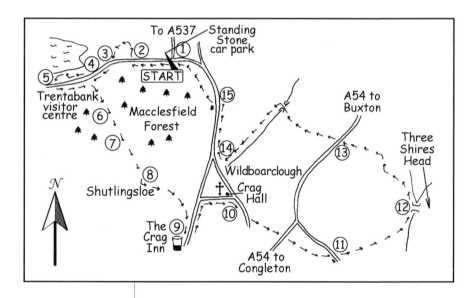

Distance:
9 miles
(3¾ miles to
the Crag Inn)

Starting point:
*Starting Stone
car park on the
eastern edge of
Macclesfield Forest.
GR 978715*

Map: OS Outdoor Leisure 24 The Peak District – White Peak Area

How to get there: *The car park lies south of the A537
between Buxton and Macclesfield. If approaching from the
east, pass the Cat & Fiddle and take the first left after
²/₃ mile. A mile later fork left at the Stanley Arms;
350 yards later fork right. Stay on this road, ignoring
another road to the right, to reach the car park on the
right just before a T-junction.*

THREE SHIRES HEAD

'*W*ilbercluff', as it's known to some locals, is right on the western fringe of the Peak District. It doesn't get the crowds that you'll find in Bakewell or Lathkill Dale and that's no bad thing. You'll be able to enjoy it a little bit more. The route is something of an 'up-and-downer' in which you climb Shutlingsloe to enjoy the views and visit Three Shires Head where the boundaries of Derbyshire, Staffordshire and Cheshire meet.

Formerly known as Bottom oth Bank, the **Crag Inn** in Wildboarclough dates back to 1629 and used to be a farm. It's a smashing pub, which even supplies plastic covers inside the porch for you to slip over your boots. That gives an idea of how popular it is with walkers. It can be a busy place at lunchtime on a Sunday, so do bear this in mind!

The food is very good – for example, half a roast duck, large king prawns, onion bhaji, grilled lamb chops – there's a real choice. That goes for the beer too, with Worthington Draught Bitter always available and guests like Cragrat,

Charles Wells' Summer Solstice and Clark's Bursting Nectar to choose from. The pub is closed on Sunday evening and all day Monday but otherwise it opens from 12 noon until 3 pm and from 7 pm until 11 pm, food being served from 12 noon until 2 pm and from 7 pm until 9 pm.

Telephone: *01260 227239.*

 *The Walk*

① From the car park, turn right along the road to the 'T'-junction. There's a memorial stone on the right in memory of 'Walter Smith 1872-1949 Historian of Macclesfield'. Cross the road and take the path to the right, which runs parallel to the lane on your right. Ahead, **Jodrell Bank** may be visible. ($^1/_4$ mile)

② After descending for some distance, cross the road to another concessionary path. Follow this as it bends right, away from the road. Turn left opposite a small pool, then left again as you follow **Forest Walk No 2**. In front of the wildlife sanctuary, turn left down some steps to the lane again. ($^1/_4$ mile)

③ Cross this to pass through a gap. Walk right (avoiding the bends) and 350 yards later pass through a gap on the right onto the road. Turn left along the road. ($^1/_4$ mile)

④ At the reservoir, beyond the layby, follow a path on the right. On reaching a gate on the left, turn right to the reservoir viewing area, which gives details of the birds you may see. Continue along the footpath to reach the **Trentabank Visitor Centre**, complete with leaflets and toilets. ($^1/_4$ mile)

⑤ With the road on your left and the **Visitor Centre** to your right, follow the path which is the start of **Forest Walks 1, 2 and 3**. After 100 yards, ignore a gravel track heading right signed for the **Forest Walks**. Continue for 50 yards parallel to the road to reach another path to the right, signposted '**Shutlingsloe**'. When this path splits take the right fork by the wall. This rises fairly steeply before levelling out a little bit. Ignore a path to the right to continue through the trees. ($^1/_2$ mile)

⑥ After passing through a kissing gate by a farmgate, turn left, still aiming for **Shutlingsloe**, and 200 yards later fork right. Pass a seat given in affectionate memory of Fred Lawton by Congleton Autumnal

Amblers. Pass through another kissing gate into the open. (¹/₄ mile)

⑦ Follow the clear path, now signed for **Wildboarclough via Shutlingsloe**. To the right is the mast on **Croker Hill** and again **Jodrell Bank** may be visible. This obvious path brings you to a rise where **Shutlingsloe** looms ahead of you. Climb a stile and turn right on the path to walk up to the trig point on the top of this hill. (³/₄ mile)

At 1,660 feet it is known as the 'Matterhorn' in the Peak District. To the left of the trig point

is a memorial to Arthur Smith, 'a doughty fighter for footpaths'.

⑧ The walk picks up a path which (as you approached it) is immediately to the right of the trig point. It descends fairly steeply towards the valley with **Crag Hall** quite prominent on the other side. Take time descending, heading in the general direction of the farm nearest to you. The path begins to curve round to the right of it. Pass through a kissing gate before crossing a footbridge. Then pass through a wall to reach the farm drive. Turn right down this for just

THE PATH UP TO SHUTLINGSLOE

under $1/2$ mile to the road.
($1 1/4$ miles)

⑨ Turn right for the **Crag Inn** and lunch. In the porch of the pub, plastic boot-covers are provided for walkers. Please use them or take off your boots. After lunch, turn left along the road, passing the driveway you descended earlier, and 75 yards later turn right over the bridge.

This bridge had to be rebuilt after the Wildboarclough Flood Disaster of 24th May 1989. A flash flood resulted in a number of bridges being damaged and a stretch of road was flooded.

Pass the delightful **Old Post Office** on the left – they don't make post offices like this any more. Go past **St Saviour's church** and continue uphill. The high wall of **Crag Hall** is plainly visible though, sadly, the Hall itself isn't. ($1/2$ mile)

⑩ Keep right, ignoring the road to the left for **Macclesfield Forest**. The road rises steeply. Where it bears right, keep straight forward, along a stony track with the **Peak & Northern** signpost for **Three Shires Head**. At the top of the track, cross a stile and continue forward beside a wall. Bear right, passing a small stone building to your right to reach a gate. Beyond this, cross some duckboarding to reach the A54. Cross this carefully to pick up the

path beyond. Aim for the far end of **Cut-thorn Edge** ahead. After passing through a wall, aim for the immediate left of the house below the Edge. The path meanders across the enclosure. ($1/2$ mile)

⑪ At the lane, turn right, then almost immediately left along a track. Follow this for $1/2$ mile to reach **Three Shires Head**. You are in Cheshire. To your right is Staffordshire and wedged in between is Derbyshire. (1 mile)

This is a point where a number of packhorse routes came together and who knows how old they are. It could well be many centuries.

⑫ Don't cross the old packhorse bridge. Stay on the left side of the stream, walking upstream. About 500 yards later, with a small valley on your left, ignore the stile on your right to pass through the gate ahead. Follow the grassy bridleway beyond alongside a fence. This rises away from the stream. Continue beside a wall in the general direction of a farm. The bridleway bears left and the farm is then across the other side of the field to your right. Pass through a gate on your right and follow the grassy track, now with the farm ahead to the right. At the end of the field, turn left (in the field) and walk uphill, keeping the wall to your right. Ignore a gap on your right after 40 yards. Ignore the first ladder-stile you see on the right leading up to the road. Climb a step-stile in the highest part of the field you're in to walk to the second ladder-stile (to the left of the first one). Climb up to the A54. ($^3/_4$ mile)

⑬ Take care at this road. Cross to the track opposite, noting the **Peak & Northern** signpost for the **Cat & Fiddle**. Follow the track for over $^1/_2$ mile as you head back towards **Macclesfield Forest**. Eventually the track leads into a valley. Keep left so that you're walking down the right side of **Cumberland Brook**. This is usually some distance below the track you're on. Continue for $^1/_2$ mile, then pass through a gate and cross a footbridge. Follow the stony track to the lane. The unmistakable shape of **Shutlingsloe** should be ahead of you. (1 mile)

⑭ Turn right at the lane. Then, at a 'T'-junction, turn right again.

Proceed along the lane, passing the **Vicarage Quarry car park**, with a picnic site opposite, next to the river. ($^3/_4$ mile)

⑮ About 450 yards beyond the quarry you reach **Dingers Hollow Farm**. Take the path immediately beyond and walk across the field, with the farmhouse immediately to your left. Pass through the gateway. Walk forward a few yards before turning right through a low gate. Walk along the green track, parallel to the road. Pass through another gate and cross the field along the line of the electricity poles. Go over a stile in a fence and head for the gate just beyond the wooden outbuilding. Cross a rather difficult stone step-stile. Turn left up the lane to turn right back to **Standing Stone car park**. ($^3/_4$ mile)

Date walk completed:

CHELMORTON TO LONGNOR

LOOKING BACK TOWARDS HIGH WHEELDON

Distance:
11¼ miles
(5¼ miles to
Longnor)

Starting point:
The main street of
Chelmorton.
GR 112699

Map: OS Outdoor Leisure 24 The Peak District – White Peak Area

How to get there: *From the A515 south-east of Buxton
turn onto the A5270. Take the first right, then the first left
to reach Chelmorton. Park 450 yards later on the road near
the War Memorial Institute on the right.*

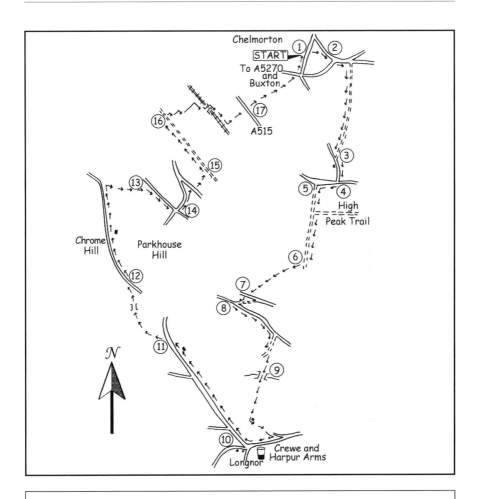

This route between Chelmorton and Longnor, between Derbyshire and Staffordshire, reveals a real contrast, as you'll see. There is a huge quarry, Hindlow, in the middle, and as the path runs along the lip of it you'll get a birds-eye view of what goes on. It is a slightly unusual walk in some respects, with plenty of very impressive scenery – Parkhouse Hill, Chrome Hill and High Wheeldon, for example. Bear in mind that the second half of the circuit is rather more testing than the first half. I tried walking it the other way but somehow it wasn't as good!

The **Crewe & Harpur Arms Hotel** stands prominent in the market place at Longnor and can't be missed. The best way for a walker to gain access is through the backdoor, which you enter from the large car park. The bar opens on Monday to Friday from 12 noon until 2 pm and from 5 pm until 11 pm. At the weekend it is open all day from 12 noon until 11 pm on Saturday and 10.30 pm on Sunday. Food is available from 12 noon until 2 pm and 5 pm until 9 pm during the week and at the weekend from 12 noon until 9 pm.

There's an interesting choice of things to eat, with specials such as deep fried cod, liver and onions and lime and chilli turkey steak, and always something for the vegetarian – Stilton and vegetable crumble, for example. Indian and Chinese dishes are also featured. Marston's Bitter and Pedigree are on tap and there's a guest beer sometimes too.

Telephone: *01298 83205.*

 # The Walk

links the Ridgeway in Buckinghamshire with the Trans Pennine Trail in Stockport.

① Walk further up the main street from the car for a short distance and take the path up the right side of the house known as **Caxterway**. Walk through the farmgates into the field beyond. Proceed up the right side of this field to a stile and the lane beyond. (¹/₄ mile)

② Turn right. At the T-junction, turn left for 120 yards, then right along the track (**Highstool Lane**, part of the **Midshires Way**). Stay on this for a mile to reach a lane. There are far-reaching views as you go. (1¹/₄ miles)

The Midshires Way is approximately 225 miles long and

③ Bear left along the lane, passing **Blinder House** (dated 1902). (¹/₂ mile)

④ At the main road look out on the right for an unusual parish boundary stone between **Chelmorton** and **Hartington Upper Quarter**. Cross the road, turn right and walk alongside it on the path between a fence and a wall. (¹/₄ mile)

⑤ After 200 yards turn left down the track. Follow this for 375 yards to reach the **High Peak Trail** on your left. Ignore this, though, and continue along the track for another 650 yards until, just beyond the crest of the hill, you cross a stile on your right. (¹/₂ mile)

⑥ Keep parallel to the wall on your right. Cross a stile and keep in the same direction, heading for the line of trees. The landscape is beginning to change now with **High Wheeldon** (1,384 feet above sea-level) ahead. Pass through the trees via a pair of stiles. Bear left down the field to climb a stile leading you into the corner of the field beyond. Head diagonally through this field, aiming for the stile just above the far corner. Follow the grassy track in the next field to reach and cross another stile. Keep in the same direction to cross a stile above the gateway. Then head to the far left corner, and 20 yards before it cross the stile onto the lane.
($^3/_4$ mile)

⑦ Cross this and climb a stile into the field below. Descend, crossing another stile onto a rough track. Turn right down this.
($^1/_4$ mile)

⑧ Turn left at the lane, passing **Abbots Grove** with its stone gateway. **High Wheeldon** is now straight ahead of you.

Opposite a quarry on the right there is a path on the left which you could follow to the top of High Wheeldon (if you want!).

After 250 yards turn right down **Green Lane**, signed

'Unsuitable for Motors'. Where the driveway you're following bears right after 200 yards, keep forward. Cross a stile, ignoring one on the left. Walk down the narrow field ahead.
($^3/_4$ mile)

⑨ Cross **Beggars Bridge** (not quite as impressive as it sounds). Walk up the field ahead, keeping straight forward. You then descend a little before rising up the right side of the stone building ahead. Turn left behind this. Pass the water troughs and bear right up the concrete track. At the end of the concrete bear left along the lane, passing houses on your right. Ignore a right turn, continue until you reach **Top o' th' Edge**. Turn right down the road into **Longnor Market Place** with the **Crewe & Harpur Arms** on the left.
($^3/_4$ mile)

Longnor is an attractive old market town, at a crossroads, not

THE CREWE & HARPUR ARMS, LONGNOR

far from the boundary with Derbyshire. It used to have an important market, as you will gather by the list of the fees payable at the top of the market place itself. Another thing that strikes you is the disproportionately high number of pubs it has. Four at the last count.

⑩ After lunch follow the main road signed '**Buxton**' and '**Glutton Bridge**' for ¹/₂ mile. Ignore the left turn for **Hollinsclough**, though there is a fine milestone here. Descend the lane past the traffic lights. (1 mile)

⑪ Pass **High Acres** and after 180 yards fork left along the lower of two driveways. At the gate to the last property, bear left along the footpath above it. In the field beyond, bear right to the footbridge in the valley. As you cross the bridge, try and guess which river you're crossing. I'll tell you later. Beyond the river, head for the rock 'column' on the left side of **Parkhouse Hill** ahead. (¹/₂ mile)

If you'd like a detour, you can climb Chrome Hill, using the concessionary path that has been negotiated.

⑫ Cross the stile onto the lane. Turn left. Ignore the driveway on the left after 20 yards and stay on the lane

to pass between **Chrome and Parkhouse Hills**. You reach **Dowall Hall**. Continue past this to enter **Dowel Dale**, still walking along the lane. After 400 yards cross the stile on your right. Zig-zag up the banking to go over a stile at the top. In the field beyond walk parallel to the wall on your left. At the far side cross the stile. Walk forward for a few yards between a pair of walls before walking down the left side of the wall on your right. Cross a stile just beyond the lowest part of the field and another on the opposite side of the track. Then head towards a stile in the far top corner of the field. (1¹/₄ miles)

⑬ Turn right on the lane beyond. Incidentally, the river you crossed earlier was the **Dove**. Pass the interestingly named '**Hatch-a-Way**'. At the crossroads, turn left (for **Buxton**) and 250 yards later, after the road has bent left, cross the stile on the right. Walk directly up the field, parallel to the fence on your left – you may have to negotiate nettles in summertime. Climb the steps up to the road. (³/₄ mile)

⑭ Turn right for 10 yards, then follow the steps through the rock garden to the step-stile at the top. Follow the (very) steep path beyond the stile, bearing gradually left. Cross another stile at the top of the field. Bear left to the fence and proceed beside it to a track at the far end. (¹/₄ mile)

⑮ Turn left along this. **Hindlow Quarry** will be to your right as you go. Some 700 yards after joining the track pass through a squeezer on your right – this is immediately before the boundary of the next quarry. (¹/₂ mile)

⑯ Walk forward with a fence on your left. At the end of the field, without passing through the field boundary, turn right. Turn left into the second field. Keep on to reach the field corner, then turn right inside the field. Turn left into the third field (for 300 yards) before turning right, with a railway line over the wall. On reaching a bridge cross this. Turn right immediately beyond. Stay beside the railway line to cross a stile, and another 10 yards later. Just over 300 yards after, cross another stile and turn left away from the railway. Near the end of the field bear slightly right to the stile leading into the trees. Pass through these to reach the A515. (1 mile)

⑰ Cross the road carefully. Take the path opposite. Continue down the left side of the field beyond. At the end of the playing field enter the first 'proper' field and head just to the right of **Chelmorton's church spire**, assuming you can see it. As you go note the trees ahead of you, running towards you. You will be passing through a stile at the nearside of these shortly. In the next field pass through the farmgate on the far side. From here bear half right to a step-stile. Then descend and ascend the valley between you and the trees mentioned earlier. Pass through the squeezer and keep forward between the trees on your left and a wall 5 yards away on your right. Once the field opens out head for the far right corner. Just before you reach the corner pass through the stile 10 yards short of it. Beyond this, and keeping in the same general direction as before, head for the far right corner of the field. Go over the road and walk up the main street in **Chelmorton**. (³/₄ mile)

Date walk completed:

YOULGREAVE, OVER HADDON AND ALPORT

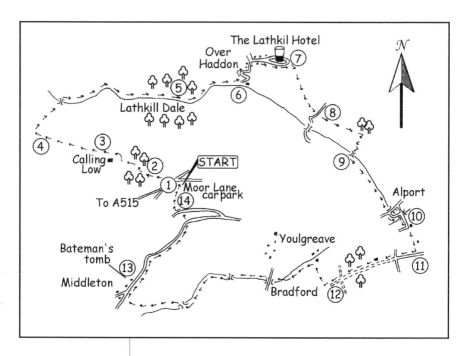

Distance:
10 miles
(4¼ miles to the Lathkil Hotel)

Starting point:
Moor Lane car park, Youlgreave.
GR 194644

Map: OS Outdoor Leisure 24 The Peak District – White Peak Area

How to get there: *From the A515 at Parsley Hay, head north for Monyash. Take the first right and follow the minor road eastwards for just under 3 miles. Then fork right to the car park (after ignoring three other right turns).*

THE RIVER LATHKILL FROM THE FIELDS ABOVE

*T*his walk passes through one of the most popular areas of the Peak District. The reason people visit it is because it's worth visiting. It's as simple as that. Lathkill Dale is a marvellous dale, changing character as you proceed. In years gone by it was an industrial landscape shaped very much by the lead miners who worked here. Fish feature on this walk, as you will see at Raper Lodge and Alport. But don't feed them please – a notice at Raper Lodge explains why not. There's a chance to visit Bateman's Tomb at Middleton in the second half of the walk.

This walk uses the **Lathkil Hotel** at Over Haddon as its watering hole – and, yes, it is 'Lathkil' with one 'L'. It's one 'L' of a pub too. Marvellous food, good beer, fine view. What more do you want? Get there early enough and (assuming the sun isn't *too* strong) try to get a window seat so you can enjoy the vista.

Walkers are requested to enter through the door on the left as you look at the frontage. Leave your boots in the corridor, then you can walk straight into the dining room, where with a bit of luck the food will already be laid out so you can see what is available. It could be steak and kidney pie or mushroom cobbler or feta and spinach quiche or roast pork among the hot dishes. As for the beers, the regulars are Whim's Hartington Bitter, Bombardier from Charles Wells and Marston's Pedigree, and there is always a guest, such as Timothy Taylor Landlord or Barnsley Bitter.

The Lathkil opens at 11.30 am (except on Sundays when it opens at 12 noon). It closes at 3 pm during the week but stays open all day at the weekend. Lunchtime food is available from opening time until 2 pm during the week and until 2.30 pm at weekends.

Telephone: 01629 812501.

 *The Walk*

NB: The concessionary path in Lathkill Dale is closed for shooting on Wednesdays between October and January.

① From the car park entrance, turn left on the lane. At the road junction cross to a stile. Following the **Limestone Way**, walk diagonally across field 1. Cross the corner of field 2. In field 3 walk vaguely parallel to the electricity lines on your left towards the trees ahead. Cross a fence into field 4, passing through a wicket gate into **Low Moor Wood**, purchased by the Peak Park in 2001 to mark the 50th Anniversary of the creation of Britain's first National Park. ($^3/_4$ mile)

② Walk along the right side of the wood to cross a stile and wicket gate into the field beyond. Head just to the right of the farm ahead. In the far corner of the field pass through a wicket gate and 100 yards later enter the wood. Keep forward to another gate 20 yards away. Cross the paddock with the farm buildings on your left. Pass through another band of trees to come out in the open. ($^1/_4$ mile)

③ The view opens out with **One Ash Grange** prominent in the valley bottom. Head for the kissing gate in front. Then, in the next field, walk towards **One Ash** to pass through a kissing gate in the bottom corner of the field. Bear slightly right to another kissing gate in the next field. The view of **Lathkill Dale** improves. Head just to the right of **One Ash** to pass through another gate. This takes you into the **Derbyshire Dales Nature Reserve**. ($^1/_2$ mile)

On the opposite side of the dale a pitched path running down from One Ash was recently washed

*away in a flash flood. The
medieval pottery that was found
amongst the debris suggests
that this was one path that
was created some centuries ago.*

④ Descend approximately 170 steps
into **Cales Dale**. Cross the stile and
bear right (and keep right) to
descend the dale. On reaching a
footbridge with a high limestone
'tor' in front, turn right beyond the
bridge to walk down **Lathkill Dale**.
After ¹/₂ mile you pass a waterfall
no more than 5 feet high but 15
yards across. It depends on the time
of year as to whether it will be
running. With a dry dale rising
uphill to the left, keep straight
forward into **Palmerston Wood**.
There are shafts and mines
hereabouts so take care. Just before
Bateman's House the path splits;
take the right fork alongside the
river. (1¹/₄ miles)

*Thomas Bateman was the
manager of Lathkill Dale Lead
Mine in the early 19th century
and his house was actually built
over a deep mineshaft.*

⑤ Continue down the dale. Just
before leaving the wood look out on
the right for a stone-lined sough
(pronounced 'suff'). This drained
water out of nearby lead mines.
As you reach the white-painted
Lathkill Lodge look out, again on
the right, for the sign referring to
the Thursday in Easter Week when a
toll of 'one penny' per person will
be charged on this path.
(1¹/₄ miles)

⑥ Bear left up the road behind
Lathkill Lodge. Zig-zag uphill to
Over Haddon, eventually passing
St Anne's church. Just beyond this
bear right at the grass triangle. Walk
through the village, bearing right

PACKHORSE BRIDGE IN BRADFORD DALE, NEAR YOULGREAVE

when the road forks to reach the **Lathkil Hotel**. ($^1/_4$ mile)

⑦ After lunch, turn left out of the pub. Pass through the stile on the tight bend 50 yards later. With your back to it, bear half right across the field, with the ground falling away 30 yards to your right. Keep in the same direction in field 2, though by now you will be above the dale. Pass through a fence on the bottom side of this field. Continue in the same direction, with a view of the river below on your right. Pass through a wicket gate. Keep straight forward, ignoring a path bearing right along the edge of the field, to pass through a stile by the gate ahead. ($^1/_2$ mile)

⑧ Cross the lane. Walk forward towards the clump of trees ahead (the ones to the right of the mast on the horizon). Resisting the temptation to take a path heading for the gateway to the right of your path, cross a step-over 70 yards to the left of the gateway. Just before reaching the trees at the far corner of the second field turn sharp(ish) right in this second field to follow the bridleroad to **Youlgreave**, walking beside the fence on your left. After reaching a gate at the end of the fence pass through it and walk forward to zig-zag down the bridleway to **Raper Bridge**, a most attractive setting with impressive trout in the water below. ($^3/_4$ mile)

⑨ Continue for 100 yards beyond the bridge and turn left through the squeezer. Walk forward with the wall on your left through nine fields to reach the road at **Alport**. Cross this towards the telephone box, noting the 1793 date on the bridge ahead. Then turn left before forking right a few yards later, passing the remains of what appears to be an old cross, to descend into the houses of **Alport**. Pass **Monks Hall** on your right. Continue to the grass triangle. Turn right over the bridge after enjoying the view of the river, especially downstream. ($^3/_4$ mile)

⑩ Continue along the lane uphill. At the sharp right-hand bend, bear left on the track beyond **Bank House**, then 50 yards later pass through a squeezer on your right and walk up the right side of the field. Climb the steps and proceed with a wall on your left to reach a step-over. Follow the short walled path to reach a drive. Turn right here to the lane. ($^1/_4$ mile)

⑪ Continue to a road junction and take the track leading uphill opposite. Pass **Millfield Lodge** on your right and all the buildings beyond it. Go through a metal squeezer just beyond the last building on your right. Follow the track on the right side of the field beyond into a wood. Keep forward on the track, ignoring others to left and right. Continue on the track beyond the wood. ($^1/_2$ mile)

⑫ At the crossroads of tracks keep forward, turning right at the end of the first field through the squeezer. Keep on the right side of the field, passing some old workings on your left. Continue forward when the path is walled, before walking on the right side of the next field. Descend into the dale beyond. Turn left on the track beside the river to reach **Bradford**. At the road keep forward, following the path running up the right side of the river, on the **Limestone Way** again. Continue beside the river to reach a lane running to the right. Cross the clapper bridge on your left and walk up the left side of the river for the next mile or so. As you go, look out for the bridge on your right 60 yards beyond a gate. Find the words engraved in it. This is one of the 'sites of meaning' marking the **Middleton parish boundary**. At the ruined sheepwash cross the river (if it's running). Continue straight up the track, ignoring a path on the left. Rise out of the dale into **Middleton**. Turn right in front of the playground. Ignoring the road leading uphill to the left, walk on the road away from the village. (2 miles)

⑬ Immediately beyond **Chapel House** (1826) turn left on a short path to **Bateman's Tomb**.

Bateman was an 18th-century archaeologist who opened many prehistoric tombs in and around Middleton. It is hoped to reinstate the tomb to something like its former glory.

Return to the lane and head left, away from **Middleton**. At the top of **Cornmill Lane** (a path descending back into **Bradford Dale**) look out on the right for the seat engraved 'In quietness and in confidence shall be your strength' – another parish boundary marker. Pass **Lomberdale Hall** on your left. At the next sharp right bend take the stile on the left and head up the **Limestone Way** to the road above. ($^3/_4$ mile)

⑭ Turn left at the road for 100 yards and follow the **Limestone Way** on your right, continuing diagonally away from the road. Zig-zag for a short distance through field 2 before straightening out. The path swings right, away from the wall to your left. At a farmgate climb the step-over and continue forward past picnic tables to the car park. ($^1/_4$ mile)

Date walk completed:

BAKEWELL, BEELEY AND CHATSWORTH PARK

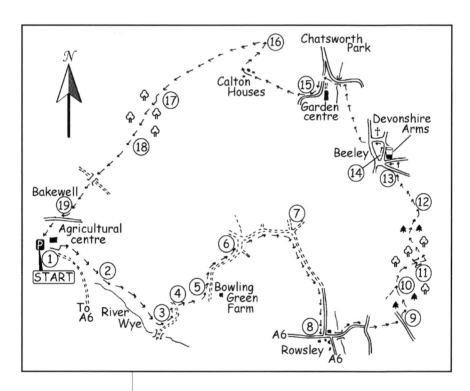

Distance:
9½ miles
(5½ miles to the Devonshire Arms)

Starting point:
Bakewell
Agricultural
Centre.
GR 222685

Map: OS Outdoor Leisure 24 The Peak District – White Peak Area

How to get there: *As you enter Bakewell from the south on the A6, turn right for the Agricultural Centre. Just before the Centre itself, as you cross a cattle grid, note the low Bakewell Show building on the left.*

BEELEY, WITH CHATSWORTH PARK BEYOND

*T*his is my BBC walk – **Bakewell-Beeley-Chatsworth** – and it's a classic. Marvellous views. Marvellous scenery. Marvellous pub. **Nuff said?**

The **Devonshire Arms** at Beeley is one of my favourite pubs. On a cold winter's day, I can think of nothing better than getting into the bar just before it starts to get busy; then I sit by the fire and order a pint of Theakston's Old Peculier – wonderful. It's pretty good in summer too. The pub is open all day, with meals available from noon.

The food, which is wide ranging and tasty, includes gammon and egg, and a delicious beef and horseradish suet pudding. If you would prefer something a bit lighter there are baguettes filled with coronation chicken or roast beef and horseradish. This very popular pub serves excellent beer too. As well as the splendid Old Peculier, there's Black Sheep Special, Black Sheep Bitter and Bass.

Telephone: *01629 733259.*

The Walk

① From the car head back to the cattle grid by the **Bakewell Show building**. Cross this and turn left to pass through the hedge a few yards away. Turn right immediately and walk beside the hedge with the showground to your left. Continue for 2/5 mile, passing through four wicket gates and keeping the hedge (or a ditch) on your right. You may notice walkers over the other side of the hedge where there is another footpath. To your left is **Manners Wood**, part of the **Haddon Estate** owned by the Dukes of Rutland who also own **Haddon Hall**. (1/2 mile)

Haddon Hall is well worth a visit if you have time later (and it's open). It's a medieval building which benefited from being 'overlooked' for centuries, possibly because Derbyshire was a little off the beaten track. It has proved very popular with film makers over the last few years.

② At an agricultural bridge over the ditch on your right, bear slightly left across the field to the corner of the hedge you've been walking beside. Cross two clapper bridges to bear right alongside the hedge again, and 300 yards later pass through another gate. Ignore the stile on the right. Walk forward through the field in front. You'll glimpse the **River Wye** on the right and possibly the odd fly fisherman. After 500 yards pass through a gate onto the tarmac lane beyond. Turn left uphill, though the **Wye** is just to the right if you want to take a closer look. (1/2 mile)

③ As you climb the lane, there are views of the river and **Haddon Fields** on the opposite side of the valley. Immediately before the lane does a sharp left turn there is a built-up tunnel through which trains used to travel underground behind **Haddon Hall**. (1/4 mile)

④ About 100 yards beyond the bend pass through a bridlegate on your right. Follow the metal fence for 500 yards to reach a track with **Bowling Green Farm** beyond. On your way you may have noticed a dovecote in the fields to your right. **Haddon Hall**, though, is usually out of sight. (1/4 mile)

⑤ Follow the track uphill as it

becomes a stony track, keeping the farm buildings on your right. After walking between hedges the view opens out on your right and **Stanton-in-Peak** and **Stanton Hall** should be visible across the valley. ($^1/_2$ mile)

⑥ Ignore a track to the right. Almost immediately there are views to the left with **Bakewell** at the far end of the valley. After 250 yards ascend a stony track to the right. **Riber Castle** may be visible 4 miles down the valley to your right. Ignore a track to the left before walking into the wood. This is quite a shady area and becomes darker the further you proceed. ($^1/_2$ mile)

⑦ About $^1/_4$ mile later, at the far corner of the wood, where a number of tracks join, bear right down the stony track, with the plantation on your right. Stay on this until it becomes a metalled lane, continuing downhill to reach the A6 beside the **Peacock Hotel**. ($^3/_4$ mile)

⑧ Turn left along the main road, cross the river and pass the **Grouse and Claret**. Where the main road does a sharp right turn, and with the road to **Chatsworth** to your left, keep forward to the path

RUSSIAN COTTAGE ON THE CHATSWORTH ESTATE

immediately to the right of the row of shops ahead. Ascend this through the stiles to reach a metal gate beneath a conifer archway. Pass through this and walk up to the **Rowsley Bar Road**. ($^1/_2$ mile)

⑨ There is a tollbar cottage up to your right but our route turns left down the lane. Just 20 yards later, turn right up a track into **Rowsley Wood**, owned by the **Haddon Estate**, and continue for 350 yards. ($^1/_2$ mile)

⑩ Fork left when the track becomes a private driveway. Ignore the path turning sharp left after a few yards. Subsequently ignore a couple of other vague paths to the left to stay on the narrow though distinct bridleway. Look out for a small horse trough on the right as you go. The bridleway narrows, with a drop to the brook on your left. Imagine riding a horse up here! ($^1/_4$ mile)

⑪ Cross a substantial wooden bridge. A few yards later, bear left downhill. Pass through a pair of large stone 'ramparts', probably used to carry spoil from **Smeltingmill Quarry** away to your right. Beyond the 'ramparts' you'll see plenty of the spoil to your left. Some 50 or 60 yards later fork right along a level path and after 100 yards bear right on a path rising uphill from the left. ($^1/_2$ mile)

⑫ At the end of the wood there's a great view ahead, with **Beeley** prominent. Keep forward, descending gently on a grassy path to a stile ahead. Continue in the same direction through the next field, passing a wall corner that juts out on the left to reach a squeezer. Walk down the right side of the field beyond this. At the bottom of the field turn right through the gate and walk beside the fence to the road. ($^1/_4$ mile)

⑬ Cross this and pass through a wicket gate. Bear slightly right across the small field to a gap. Follow the path before swinging left downhill to cross a stream. On the lane beyond, turn left beside the brook. As you reach the **Devonshire Arms**, note the lane to the right. This is the one you will follow after your pub lunch. ($^1/_4$ mile)

Beeley is part of the Chatsworth Estate like Edensor and Pilsley at the other end of Chatsworth Park. It shares a similar style of building in some cases with Edensor and, of course, the same Chatsworth 'blue'.

⑭ After you've eaten, proceed up the lane mentioned in the previous paragraph to reach a grass triangle. Keep left here on the road, then swing left to pass the church to your right to reach the main road. Cross this, pass through the kissing gate and turn right for ¹/₂ mile through the field. Turn left over the bridge on the far side of the field. Pass the house on the left and rise up the bank beyond to reach the entrance to **Chatsworth Garden Centre**. Cross this to turn left just a few yards later along a 'No Thro' Road'. You then pass the garden centre over the wall on your left before swinging right into **Calton Lees**. This is also part of the **Derwent Valley Heritage Way**, though you now leave it! (1 mile)

⑮ At a small grass triangle, bear right and pass through the middle gate of three farmgates. Ascend the track beyond for ³/₄ mile to reach **Calton Houses**, just two or three properties. Stay on the bridleway between the houses. Pass through a gate into the open. Turn right beside a wall for 200 yards. At the end of the wall continue along the track, rising gently for 150 yards. (1 mile)

⑯ Turn left along another track and ¹/₃ mile later pass through a farmgate. Keep forward towards the highest point ahead. This will bring you alongside a fence on your left. Cross the stile beside a gate, with a

pond 20 yards beyond it. Keep to the left of this to cross another stile. From here (with your back to the stile) bear half left for **Bakewell**, keeping just to the left of the ring-fenced trees. Head for the lowest part of the field. (1 mile)

⑰ Pass through a wicket-gate into the wood and descend the steepish path beyond. At a cross path turn right for a few yards, then by the breeze block 'construction' turn left down a rocky path. On reaching **Haddon Estate's** concessionary path on the left, bear right downhill. (¹/₄ mile)

⑱ At the edge of the golf course proceed forward – look out for flying golf balls! On reaching a fenced track, follow this to cross a bridge over the **Monsal Trail**. Walk down the left side of the field beyond. Pass through a gate and follow the driveway to **Coombs Road**. (¹/₂ mile)

⑲ Turn right here. Then turn left immediately beyond **Long Meadow House**. The **Agricultural Centre** is then in front of you. (¹/₄ mile)

Date walk completed:

ROWSLEY, DARLEY BRIDGE AND THE DERWENT VALLEY

THE THREE STAGS HEADS, DARLEY BRIDGE

Distance:
9$^1/_2$ miles
(5$^1/_4$ miles to the Three Stags Heads)

Starting point:
Rowsley Recreation Ground.
GR 256656

Map: OS Outdoor Leisure 24 The Peak District – White Peak Area

How to get there: *From the A6 in Rowsley, turn onto School Lane opposite the Peacock. The Recreation Ground is just beyond the bridge. Park at the roadside.*

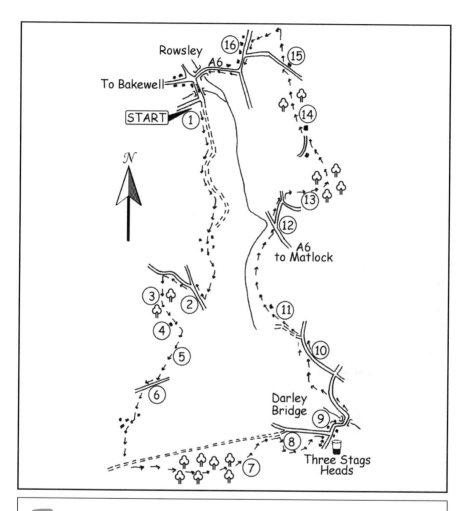

The Derwent Valley Heritage Way was launched in 2003 and the second part of this route gives you an opportunity to follow at least some of it. It has to be said, though, that for most of the walk you'll be looking down at the Derwent Valley. This is an enjoyable, varied medium distance circuit and includes some permissive paths just before you reach the Three Stags Heads at Darley Bridge. On the way back enjoy the Derwent Valley itself, and if it's the weekend look out for one of Peak Rail's steam trains chugging up the line.

This is a 'friendly family pub' according to the landlord, and I wouldn't disagree with that. The **Three Stags Heads** at Darley Bridge opens on Monday to Friday from 12 noon until 3 pm and 6.30 pm until 11 pm. On Saturday it is open from 12 noon until 11 pm and on Sunday from 12 noon until 10.30 pm. The pub used to be the home of the local stag hunt hence the 'GOQ' above the door. It is supposed to mean 'Go Out Quietly'. I'm told the deer that are prevalent in this area are Norwegian roe deer.

Hardys & Hansons Bitter plus a guest like Frolicking Farmer, Guzzling Goose or Peddlars Pride are on offer, also plenty of tempting culinary treats as well as a variety of bar snacks. Dishes such as pork steak in plum sauce, chicken à la Romana and lemon peppercorn chicken will whet your appetite.

Telephone: *01629 732358.*

The Walk

① From the roadside, walk back towards the roadbridge. Before crossing it turn right along the lane for **Stanton Woodhouse**. Initially level, the lane then rises, zig-zagging through **Holly Wood**. Continue for 100 yards, then take the path on the right. Walk up the left side of the field beyond. Leave the field by a gate, bearing right uphill on the track. Stay on this between the buildings to reach a farmgate at the far end. Pass into the field beyond and 30 yards later ascend the grassy track. This bears right and reaches a pair of gates. Take the one on the left and 20 yards later bear diagonally slightly left off the track along the path to reach a small gate. Walk along the fenced path. Continue forward, eventually bearing right to reach the lane via a step-stile (1¹/₂ miles)

② Turn right on the lane, then left (for **Stanton-in-Peak**) at a junction 300 yards later. After 400 yards climb the step-stile on the left, 20 yards before the road bends right. (If you reach the entrance to the quarry on your right you've gone too far.) Walk to the wood at the top of the field, keeping parallel to the trees on your right. (¹/₂ mile)

③ The path should lead through the centre of the wood, but most people seem to walk up the right side. Where the field on your right ends, keep forward. You will soon be walking between a fence on your right and a quarry down to your left. Ignore the stile in the fence on your right. (If you wish to visit the **Nine Ladies Stone Circle** follow the path beyond the stile for 150 yards or so.) Keep alongside the fence on your right. (¹/₄ mile)

④ You reach the **Reform Tower** and enter the National Trust property of **Stanton Moor Edge**. Continue along the edge of the moor. When the fence and path swing right follow them, but not before you've walked forward for 20 yards to visit the **Cat Stone** (engraved 'EIN 1831'). (¹/₄ mile)

The tower was built in 1832 and marked Earl Grey's contribution towards the Reform Act. It is not open to the public, which seems a great pity. What a view it must give. The Peak Park is in the process of cutting down some of the number of silver birches growing on the moor. These tend to 'swamp' the heather, which dies back as a result.

⑤ Stay on the main path round the edge of the moor with marvellous views down the **Derwent Valley** towards **Matlock** and **Riber Castle**. Ignore a stile on the right near the National Trust sign. Keep forward, descending gradually to the lane. In summertime this path can

be quite overgrown. (¹/₂ mile)

⑥ Turn right for 200 yards. Take the path on the left and follow this, staying on the left side of the field as you near the buildings ahead. Pass one building on your left, keeping the others on your right. Bear right immediately past **Hill Carr Barn**. At a farmgate proceed along the right side of the two fields beyond to reach **Clough Lane**. Turn left along this track for 400 yards. Then pass through a squeezer on the right. Bear left through the field, initially keeping the wall at the top of the field no more than 25 yards away. This path used to be a track leading into the wood. Enter **Clough Wood** and stay on this for ¹/₂ mile. The wood is full of deer and at dusk you'll be unlucky not to see some. (1¹/₂ miles)

THE REMAINS OF MILLCLOSE MINE, NEAR DARLEY BRIDGE

⑦ Eventually the path comes out in the open. A few yards later, you reach the remains of **Millclose Mine**. In front of the large stone arch is a capped shaft hundreds of feet deep. Proceed on the path to reach a track rising from the right. Turn left on this and then keep right to walk down the lane with Enthoven's tall chimney some 200 feet above you on your left. (1/4 mile)

Thanks are due to H.J. Enthoven & Sons who have created some permissive paths, which are used on this walk.

⑧ About 50 yards before the road junction, turn right over the stile by the double gates. Follow the track beyond through the trees to bear right, then left down to a stream. Don't cross this; turn left alongside it. Walk downstream to enter a limestone 'gorge'. There's a pond on the right. Just beyond the path forks. Ignore the right fork and keep forward underneath the trees again. Some 40 yards before the road fork right. Cross a footbridge and keep forward, passing through a kissing gate to the road. Turn right to the **Three Stags Heads**. (1/2 mile)

⑨ After lunch, turn right out of the pub and follow the road over the **Derwent**, passing the **Square and Compass** to reach the picnic site. Immediately before the picnic site

turn left, with the cricket ground on your left. This is part of the **Derwent Valley Heritage Way**. Pass the scoreboard. Keep into the field beyond. **Stanton Moor** is straight ahead and hopefully it's in focus after your lunchtime stop. Stay on the right side of the field for 350 yards. Pass through the stile on your right. In the field beyond keep to the left of the kennels to reach the far left corner. (3/4 mile)

⑩ Turn left at the road and visit **St Helen's church** with the **Darley Yew** (said to be 2,000 years old). Fork left beyond the church on the cul-de-sac, still following the **Derwent Valley Heritage Way**. Keep forward past the primary school and go through the gate of **The Abbey House**. Keep on the main driveway through all the buildings. Where the drive swings right, keep forward through a squeezer and shortly afterwards a step-over. (1/4 mile)

⑪ Walk on the right side of the field beyond to the stone outbuilding. Beyond this keep forward to the gate ahead. In the next field walk forward to the *far* gate, not the nearest one; ignore a stile on your right just beyond the nearest gate too. Walk past the 'stranded' hedge to the gate beyond. The path then runs along the left side of a hedge to bring you to the river. Walk forward with this on your left to reach **Nanny Goat Crossing**. Cross railway lines to reach the A6. (1 mile)

⑫ Turn left, use the pelican crossing and proceed up **Northwood Lane** for 200 yards. Where the road turns right uphill, bear left for 20 yards before turning right into the lorry park. Head up through this, keeping to the left of the buildings on the right. Head for the top right-hand corner and enter the field beyond. Keep up the right side of this to enter **Northwood Carr** by the stile to the left of the water trough. (¹/₄ mile)

⑬ Follow the path, rising through the wood. Ignore any minor paths, though 300 yards later swing left uphill where the path forks. You reach a bridleway. Turn left to reach a field on your left after 100 yards. Continue along the edge of the wood. Proceed along the level path ahead to reach another gate. Walk to the lane beyond and turn right uphill. Pass through the gateway at **Tinkersley Farm**, keeping to the left of a wooden building to enter a field. Head through the field on the

level path to enter **Copy Wood**. (¹/₂ mile)

⑭ Proceed on the path through the wood for 500 yards. At the end of the wood keep in the same direction between two lines of trees crossing a small private golf course. (¹/₂ mile)

⑮ On reaching the road turn left downhill for 100 yards. Turn right on the track into **Rowsley Wood** and 350 yards later fork left off the track, then go sharp left on the footpath within 10 yards. Follow this down to the road. (¹/₂ mile)

As I strim this footpath every summer (as a member of the Derbyshire Dales Group of the Ramblers' Association) I hereby promise that I will endeavour to keep this path clear! If I'm hard at it as you pass by feel free to have a word.

⑯ Turn left at the road and proceed to the A6. Turn right here, subsequently crossing the **River Derwent**. Just beyond this bear left into **School Lane** to return to your car. (¹/₂ mile)

Date walk completed:

TITTESWORTH RESERVOIR, THE ROACHES AND MEERBROOK

THE ROACHES FROM TITTESWORTH RESERVOIR

Distance:
10³/₄ miles
(6 miles to the
Lazy Trout)

Starting point:
A small car park
between the A53
and Tittesworth
Reservoir.
GR 999603

Map: OS Outdoor Leisure 24 The Peak District – White Peak Area

How to get there: *From the A53 between Leek and Buxton, turn off westwards at the sign for Tittesworth Reservoir. Just over ¹/₂ mile later cross a roadbridge and turn left almost immediately into a small car park.*

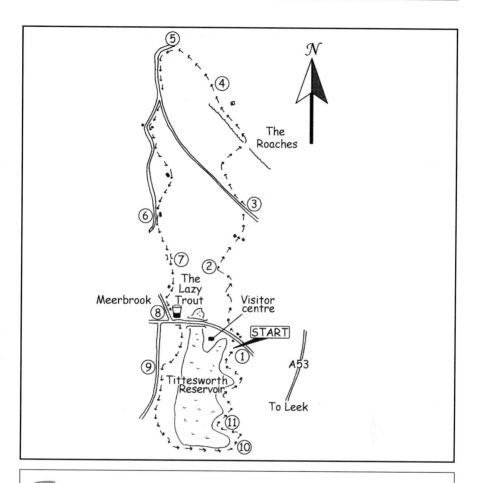

*T*his is a walk of two halves. The first half is in and around the rough and rugged Roaches with far-reaching views (weather permitting); the second half is an interesting circuit of Severn Trent Water's Tittesworth Reservoir, so take your binoculars. After the walk and your lunchtime stop at the Lazy Trout why not spend some time at Severn Trent's Tittesworth Reservoir Visitor Centre? There is plenty to do. It has a shop, a restaurant (so you can have tea there!) and an exhibition area, as well as outdoor features such as a barbecue area, a children's play area, a sensory garden, a couple of bird hides and a feeding station. It's well worth visiting.

The view from the beer garden of the **Lazy Trout** in Meerbrook must be one of the best in the country. Sit there on a warm summer's day and enjoy it whilst cooling down with a pint of beer. They serve Banks's Bitter as well as Pedigree and a guest such as Marston's Sweet Chariot. There's a good choice of food too, with their pies being particularly popular. There's much more, though – you might be tempted by the Staffordshire oatcakes with cheese and onion filling, or mushroom, or perhaps bacon and egg. If the weather's not so good then you'll be pleased to read that it's just as nice inside as out.

Food is available from 12 noon until 2.30 pm at weekends and in the week from 11.30 am to 2 pm. Please note that the Lazy Trout is not open on Tuesdays.

Telephone: *01538 300385.*

The Walk

① Turn left along the road. Pass **Middle Hulme Farm**. On the left note the 1758 date stone on the house. Ignore a track on the right and 60 yards later take the path on the right. Head across field 1, aiming for the hollow between **The Roaches** and **Hen Cloud**. Head across field 2 and keep in the same direction across field 3. Head directly across field 4. On reaching the fence turn right and walk alongside it, then 100 yards later turn left, crossing a footbridge. Bear half right across field 5. Cross field 6 to a gate tucked away behind a holly tree. In field 7 walk forward alongside the fence on your right. (³/₄ mile)

② After 200 yards pass through a squeezer on your right. Walk up the left side of the field beyond, then the right side of the next field. On reaching a barn pass through a squeezer and bear steadily right to the left-hand side of the farm ahead. Follow the path to the right (between a holly hedge and a breeze block building), bringing you into the farmyard. Bear left to the farmgate at the top. This gives you an opportunity to admire **Windygates Farmhouse**. About 40 yards beyond the gate take the steps on the left. Walk up the left side of the field to the lane. (³/₄ mile)

③ Turn left for 300 yards. Pass through the gate at **Roaches Gate**, bearing left immediately along a sunken lane. After 350 yards the path swings right. Almost immediately you should follow some small steps up the banking in front. These take you up the right side of a quarry. At the top proceed along another sunken path. Stay on this as it levels out. Head towards a gateway and the trees beyond. Follow the obvious path forward, bearing slightly right uphill. Pass through a 'nick' in the rocks. Turn left as soon as possible, alongside a tumble-down wall on your left. Proceed on the main, stone-pitched, path. **Doxey Pool** is reached. (1 mile)

There's supposed to be something malevolent in Doxey Pool so be careful nothing grabs your ankle as you pass by. 'The Roaches' originates from the French 'Roches' meaning 'rocks' – we actually pass Roche Grange later.

④ Beyond **Doxey Pool** continue with the 'drop' on your left. Over 3/4 mile later a trig point is reached. Then about 1/2 mile later you reach a road. (1 1/4 miles)

⑤ Turn left down this for just over 1/2 mile. Fork right down the lane for **Meerbrook** and 400 yards later pass **Roche Grange**. Some 300 yards after this take a path on the left (on a right-hand bend). Walk

WALKING THROUGH THE WOODLAND NEAR TITTESWORTH RESERVOIR

along the left side of the first two fields before going directly across the third. Cross a step-over and bear right towards the far side of the house (keeping the house on your right). Beyond the house cross the step-over in the wall on your right. In the paddock beyond keep parallel to the fence on your right. Climb a stile by the gate. Proceed parallel to the drive on your right to reach another step-over. Bear *slightly* left across the field in front to reach a stile by a tall tree. Head down the field beyond to a stile in the far field boundary. After this, head forward to a stile 15 yards to the left of the right end of the garden fence. Cross the corner of the lawn to reach the lane beyond. ($1^3/_4$ miles)

⑥ Turn left to pass the property and 30 yards beyond the right-hand bend, cross a step-over on the left and another a few yards later. Stay parallel to the hedge on the left to walk through the first field. Keep in the same direction in the second field to reach a bridge. ($^1/_4$ mile)

⑦ Head in the direction the bridge is pointing, to the far left corner of the field. Climb a step-over and turn left between the hedge and fence. Cross a small bridge and walk forward on the left side of the field beyond. Cross a track and climb a stile. Bear slightly right to climb a step-over 50 yards away. Walk forward alongside a hedge on the right for 200 yards, then cross the fence on your right and head diagonally left across a paddock to the gateway beyond the house. Turn right along the walled track, with the property to your right. Continue along the drive to the road. Turn left here into **Meerbrook** to reach the **Lazy Trout**. ($^1/_2$ mile)

⑧ After lunch, turn left along the road towards the reservoir. About 100 yards beyond the Methodist chapel take the path described as '**Long Trail**' on the right. Stay on the obvious path, with the reservoir on your left. On reaching the fishermen's car park, turn right up the access road to the road proper. (1 mile)

⑨ Turn left for 400 yards, then left again over the cattle grid (signed '**Long Trail**' again). Stay on this subsequently to cross a cattle grid, ignoring a footpath to the right, to walk through **North Hillswood Farm**. Beyond this, proceed alongside a wood on your right. On the other side of the wood look out on your left for another '**Long Trail**' sign. Take this and head into the trees. Steps lead down to the reservoir wall. ($1^1/_4$ miles)

⑩ On the far side of the wall, keep forward, climbing the steps into the trees. Stay on the meandering path through the wood for some way (as you go, ignore a stile on the right leading into a field). A stile on the path brings you more into the open before you descend steps into a wooded valley. Here you cross a stream by a footbridge and swing left back towards the reservoir. You'll see the reservoir wall soon and realise you haven't gone very far as the crow flies. (¹/₂ mile)

⑪ The footpath veers away from the reservoir again and you enter a conifer plantation before walking alongside an open field on the right. Duckboarding leads you back into the trees and, after descending various steps and crossing a few footbridges, you come out into the open again. Proceed on the path, with the reservoir on your left. The **Visitor Centre** will be visible as you go. Subsequently enter a wood,

where the path is surfaced with gravel. Just after crossing a stream, fork right along some boarding to follow the '**Long Trail**'. Cross another stream before ignoring a sharp right turn leading to a gate with **The Roaches** beyond. On joining another gravel path, turn right with **The Roaches** on the horizon to your right. Keep on this path towards **The Roaches**, crossing some open ground as you go. Enter another wood and cross a wide wooden bridge shortly after, followed by another. Beyond this there is a picnic area. Fork right here along a tarmac path (keeping a stream on your right) to reach the car park. (1³/₄ miles)

Date walk completed:

HULME END, ECTON HILL AND BUTTERTON

LOOKING BACK AT ECTON FROM ECTON HILL

Distance:
8 miles
(4³/₄ miles to the Black Lion)

Starting point:
Hulme End Visitor Centre.
GR 103593

Map: OS Outdoor Leisure 24 The Peak District – White Peak Area

How to get there: *Hulme End is 2 miles south-west of Hartington on the B5054, which runs between the A155 and the B5053 at Warslow. The Visitor Centre is on the left.*

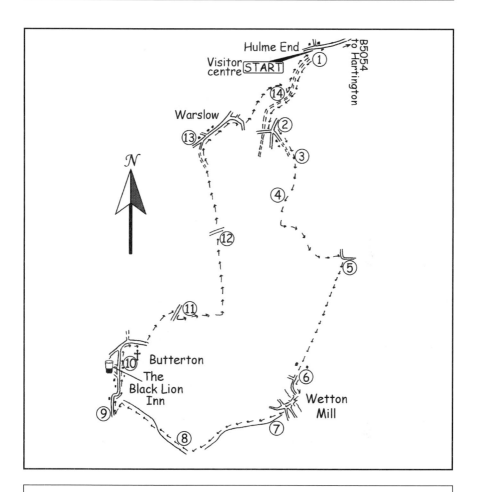

There is a lot of impressive scenery on this walk in Staffordshire, an underrated county scenery-wise. This isn't a route for those who are a bit nervous of heights – the path across Ecton Hill, whilst giving absolutely stunning views, ascends a steeply sloping bank. It's safe enough, however, as long as it's not icy underfoot. Later you can enjoy a gentler ramble beside Hoo Brook before visiting Butterton, where part of the main village street is a ford and drivers are warned to take care and look out for ducks in the road. You return, as you set out, along the Manifold Way.

The **Black Lion Inn** ('and Ale House' to give it its full name) is in the middle of Butterton, and a more characterful pub you'd be hard pressed to find. It has low ceilings, good food and excellent beer. There are usually five ales to choose from: Theakston Best Bitter plus others such as Young's Special Premium Ale, John Smith's Magnet, John Smith's Extra Smooth and Everard's Mild.

It's all right to wear boots in the walkers' bar to the left as you enter. Now what's the story behind the giant wooden clothes peg hanging outside the pub? I know, but perhaps I'd better not let it out of the bag.

You'll enjoy studying the menu with its varied range of dishes – among them spinach and ricotta cannelloni, Brie rosti, cod and prawn crumble. The Black Lion serves food each weekday (except Monday) from 12 noon until 2 pm and at weekends from 12 noon until 3 pm. In the evenings food is available from 7 pm until 9 pm.

Telephone: *01538 304232.*

① Walk along the **Manifold Way** away from the **Visitor Centre**. After $1/2$ mile it crosses over the river and 400 yards later you reach a lane. You will be walking across **Ecton Hill**, which rises above you, later. ($3/4$ mile)

The Manifold Way runs along what used to be the Leek and Manifold Light Railway. What a picture it must have been, steam engines chugging through this lovely landscape.

② Turn left at the lane, then right, then almost immediately left uphill on the track signed '**Top of Ecton**'

and '**Wetton**'. Pass various houses on the left and continue to the right of the building (dated 1931 and engraved 'AR') with the green spire. Continue through the buildings, passing under a stone 'bridge'. Turn left on the path immediately beyond this. Climb the steps and turn right along the path beside a wall. ($1/4$ mile)

Ecton is well known for the copper mines that used to exist here. They were owned by the Dukes of Devonshire and it is said that the profits from the mines financed the building of The Crescent in Buxton.

③ Keep forward along the grassy path, which rises steadily across the hillside ahead. With the road and an old quarry below to your right, you ascend fairly steadily. Ignore all paths crossing or joining the one you are on. This path is like many things in life, it's easier doing it than thinking about it! ($^1/_4$ mile)

④ The path levels out with a 180 degree view. **Grindon church spire** is to the left, **Butterton's spire** to the right of it, **Warslow** ahead of you and **Ecton Hill** on your right. Follow the levelish path with **Swainsley** down to your right. To the left of it is a dovecote beside the **River Manifold**. Just before reaching a line of hawthorns ahead of you, bear left uphill to a stile. Cross this, heading directly forward up the field in front, and 110 yards later you reach a wall corner jutting into the field. Bear half right here and pass through a gateway 140 yards away. Beyond this, walk diagonally across the field (on a cattle track) to the bottom right corner. Climb the step-over and turn left towards the lane ahead. Cross the stile in the bottom corner of the field. Bear right along the lane. ($^1/_2$ mile)

⑤ After 30 yards pass through a wicket gate on your right. Walk down the field beside a wall on your right. Do the same in field 2. In field 3, continue down the dale but with the wall now on your left. Don't stray far from the wall because at the end of the field you need to walk beside a fence to enter field 4. At the end of field 4, cross a stile into the National Trust property, **Dale Farm**. Just 25 yards later turn left over a step-over and descend. In front of you is the **Sugarloaf** though it will look more like a loaf in 10 minutes if you look back. After a steep descent beside the **Sugarloaf** you reach a grassy dale-bottom. Keep forward, ignoring a track forking right as you proceed, and 500 yards beyond the **Sugarloaf** (did you look back?) you reach **Dale Farm** itself. Cross the step-over behind the farmhouse and walk forward through the farmyard. (1 mile)

BUTTERTON

⑥ Continue forward on the track ahead, ignoring the track on the right. You reach **Wetton Mill**, where there are toilets and a tearoom. Cross the roadbridge on your right. Keep forward, crossing the tarmac lane before bearing right, with a ford on your left, to pass through a gate signed as a public bridleway. ($^1/_4$ mile)

⑦ Walk up the valley, with the lane over the hedge on your right. Aim for the right-hand of two gates. **Ossom's Hill** is on your left and **Hoo Bank** on your right. Continue on the gravel path in the second field. Stay in the valley bottom on the obvious path and $^3/_4$ mile after leaving **Wetton Mill** you reach a small footbridge. Take the stile on the right signposted '**Butterton**'. ($^3/_4$ mile)

⑧ About 200 yards later in the first field pass through the stile on your left. Look carefully for this. Don't rise up the hillside as the stile *is* in the valley bottom. Continue for another 300 yards through a number of fields, with the stream on your left. Go over the stream by some almost non-existent stepping stones and continue up the main valley (crossing a smaller stream) for $^1/_2$ mile, with **Hoo Brook** now on your right. As you reach **Butterton**, cross a step-over, walking beside the brook. At the far end of the small 'enclosure', squeeeeeeze through a

stile. Walk up the field beyond to a gate at the top. Pass through the stile and turn right onto the lane. ($^3/_4$ mile)

⑨ Turn right down this to a ford. Follow the cobbled lane, looking out for ducks as you go. Pass **Brookside Cottage** on the left. Beyond the ford, bear right uphill, then left at **The Old School**. When the road forks 150 yards later, take the right fork to the **Black Lion Inn**. ($^1/_4$ mile)

⑩ After lunch, turn left up the lane and follow it round to the right, walking beside the churchyard on your right. Ignore a track to the left as you go. Just 10 yards beyond the end of the churchyard, climb a step-over on the left. With your back to this, head half right across the field. In field 2 walk towards a red barn with **Warslow** beyond. Pass through the stile in the lowest corner of this field. Walk along the bottom side of field 3, cutting the very small corner of field 4. Turn right to walk along the right side of field 5 and 50 yards later enter field 6 through the gate. Walk down the left side of this field, bearing right towards the far end to pass through a squeezer onto the lane. ($^1/_2$ mile)

⑪ Turn right for 30 yards, then left through a squeezer and walk beside the hedge on your right for 200 yards. At the end of the field, climb the step-over to the left of the field corner. Cross the narrow second and third fields before bearing slightly left to a step-over beyond a narrow clapper bridge. Turn right beyond this to walk beside the stream and cross another step-over below the stone barn. In the next field head forward, aiming 50 yards to the left of the bottom corner of the field. On reaching the hedge, turn left uphill with the hedge on your right to reach a bridlegate. Cross this and walk across the field to another bridlegate. Proceed along the gravel lane beyond to a lane. ($^1/_2$ mile)

⑫ Pass through the bridlegate ahead and walk down the rocky bridleway into the valley. On reaching **Warslow Brook** feel free to paddle across it (or go over on the bridge). In the field beyond walk up the left side of the hedge to the bridlegate in the top right corner. Follow the hedged bridleway beyond. This brings you to a property where the bridleway passes between the two houses (or you could follow the 'Alternative Footpath' to the left). Head up the drive away from the houses and continue forward on the tarmac lane

as it winds its way for $^1/_3$ mile to reach the main road in **Warslow**. ($^3/_4$ mile)

⑬ Turn right along this road for 300 yards, leaving **Warslow**. Turn right for **Ecton** and 250 yards later ignore a lane to the left. Some 150 yards after this (on a right-hand bend) pass through the squeezer in front. *Ignore the grassy track ahead*, instead follow the path *alongside* the wall on your left. About 100 yards later, with an old quarry to the left, keep forward along the grassy path, with the wall away to your left. Soon you'll be walking alongside a hawthorn hedge on your left with the **Manifold Way** below to your right. Keep forward on the obvious (narrow) path, with a drop to your right. Climb a step-over. Gradually the path loses height; but with the field boundary to your left there shouldn't be many problems. Just before reaching the **Manifold Way** the path descends more steeply and does a sharp right to the Way itself. (1 mile)

⑭ Turn left along the **Manifold Way** back to the start. ($^1/_2$ mile)

Date walk completed:

ALSOP EN LE DALE, BIGGIN AND THE TISSINGTON TRAIL

BIGGIN DALE

Distance:
9 miles
(4³/₄ miles to
the Waterloo)

Starting point:
*Alsop car park on
the Tissington Trail.
GR 156549*

Map: OS Outdoor Leisure 24 The Peak District – White Peak Area

How to get there: *Alsop en le Dale lies just east of the
A515 between Ashbourne and Buxton. Approaching from
the south, the old station car park is on the right, a couple
of miles beyond the Tissington turn.*

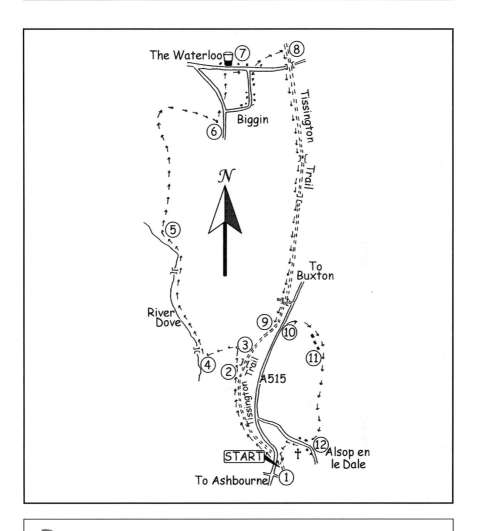

*D*elightful White Peak scenery is the order of the day with a chance to walk in both Dovedale and Biggin Dale. The section of Dovedale you'll be passing through is likely to be a bit quieter than the stretch a mile or two downstream as the car park is down that end. After lunch, a steady return along the Tissington Trail gives you a chance to build up your energy before visiting Alsop en le Dale (and climbing back up to the car park).

The **Waterloo Inn** at Biggin by Hartington has opening times that will suit the walker who needs a bit of leeway as regards when he or she want to eat. It is open on Monday to Thursday from 11 am until 4 pm and 6.30 pm until 11 pm. Then on Friday and Saturday it opens from 11 am until 11 pm; on Sunday from 12 noon to 10.30 pm. Food is available every day from 12 noon until 3 pm and 6.30 pm until 9 pm.

The menu offers plenty of choice – quarter pounder burger or double burger (plus salad plus fries) for those who want something simple. Or what about a soup and roll? Fancy something a bit more oriental? Then try dim sum. Something hot? Try japaleno peppers. There are some interesting sounding specials on the blackboard too – lamb rogan josh, rice and poppadum as well as chicken jalfrezi. Vegetarian dishes are also available.

You will probably need something to wash all this down so the beers to choose from are important. Black Sheep Best and Black Sheep Special are on tap, and there is usually a guest such as Timothy Taylor Landlord or Theakston Draught Mild.

Telephone: *01298 84284.*

① Walk onto the **Tissington Trail** at the back of the car park and turn left. After a couple of hundred yards, pass under the A515. Continue on the Trail for ³/₄ mile, ignoring a path on the left as you go. Just before the Trail passes above an agricultural track via a bridge, take the footpath on the left leading down to the track. Cross the track and pass through the small gate onto **Bradbury's Bank**. (1 mile)

② With your back to the gate walk half right, aiming for **Johnson's**

Knoll, a tree-topped hill. As you walk across the field, there's a slight 'bump' on your right, the remains of **Nettly Knowe**, an ancient barrow chopped in half when the railway was built.

③ Pass through a gap on the far side of the field. Suddenly the path (popular with sheep) descends fairly steeply into the dale.

There's a line of thought that most paths started out as animal trails centuries ago. Quite whether walkers follow sheep, or vice versa, on this path is debatable!

In the bottom of the dale, turn left and descend it. After ¹/₂ mile you reach the **River Dove** near **Coldeaton Bridge**. Now is a good time to stop and sample the splendid scenery, the sounds of the river, the wildlife. Chances are that a white-bibbed dipper will be somewhere in the river. (³/₄ mile)

④ Turn right upstream. After 50 yards, you pass **Coldeaton Bridge** on your left. With the river still on your left, the path runs in the shade of the wood on your right. Eventually you reach the small **Iron Tors pumphouse**. This was built to pump water to farmland above. On the left at this point is the **Gypsy Bank footbridge**. This was built

recently to allow walkers to cross the **Dove** when the water level was up. The stepping stones are about ten yards downstream of the bridge. Try to imagine crossing them when the river was high! Continue upstream to pass through a squeezer 15 yards later. Less than 200 yards after this, pass through another squeezer. Turn right now to leave the **River Dove** behind. (³/₄ mile)

⑤ This takes you into **Biggin Hill**, a dry grassy dale which you follow for over a mile. In the dale is the **Biggin Dale Nature Reserve** forming part of the **Derbyshire Dales National Nature Reserve**,

THE WATERLOO INN, BIGGIN

particularly important for its flora. On reaching a dew pond over the wall on the left, you will see a bridleway on the left to **Hartington**, but please follow the bridleway to the right – to **Dalehead**. Keep in the valley bottom as you proceed. This one is dry too. Just under $1/2$ mile later you reach the top end of the dale. Here you should head forward, keeping the electricity lines on your right. ($1^3/4$ miles)

⑥ At the road turn left for 250 yards. Ignore the right turn into **Drury Lane**. Just under 250 yards later take the footpath on your right, aiming for the field corner jutting out into the field ahead. Walk down the left side of the field beyond. In the field before the road, bear slightly right to the wicket gate with the **Waterloo Inn** just to the right. Head for the pub once you're on the road. ($1/2$ mile)

⑦ After a stop turn left up the road through **Biggin**. Ignore **Drury Lane** again – the other end this time – and 75 yards later take the footpath on the left between the houses. Walk along the left-hand side of the first field, head to the far corner of the second field, then in the third keep on the right side to reach the **Tissington Trail**. Climbing up the steps, turn right to walk on the Trail for a couple of miles. ($1/2$ mile)

The Tissington Trail leaves

Ashbourne through an impressive tunnel and 13 miles later links up with the High Peak Trail at Parsley Hay. It is open to cyclists and walkers.

⑧ The Trail is particularly enjoyable hereabouts because of the views from it. As you go, cross the road leading into **Biggin**. A sign on the left immediately beyond denotes that the slope is 1 in 330. In the cuttings where there are no far-reaching views, there are habitats in miniature with lots of wildflowers in summer. Cross over **Back Lane** (with grass in the middle of it). The Trail then passes under a high bridge linking one set of fields with another. It subsequently crosses **Liffs Road** as the A515 on your left converges with it. (2 miles)

⑨ About 400 yards beyond **Liffs Road** there's a layby beside the A515. Hereabouts you should take one of a pair of paths that lead out near the north-eastern point of the layby.

⑩ Cross the road and head along the dead-end road to the left of the layby. This leads to **Alsop Moor Cottages**, six pairs of semi-detached properties in a pleasant rural setting. ($1/2$ mile)

⑪ Walk for 80 yards beyond the last house and pass through the squeezer stile on your right. In the first field head diagonally to the far corner. Cross the corner of the second field before keeping in the same direction in the third field. In the third field the path passes through a gateway by a trough. Head for the squeezer in the far left corner of the fourth field before entering a large fifth field. As you enter this field there's a walled group of trees ahead to the right. Proceed along the wall on your left until you reach the corner. Then bear half left, steadily walking away from the wall. A view opens up of the village of **Alsop en le Dale** ahead of you. **Cross Low** is to your left.

Within a few miles of this spot are quite a collection of 'lows'. The OS White Peak map shows End Low, Aleck Low, Hawks Low, Minninglow, The Low, Moat Low, Stand Low and Steep Low. All are said to be the burial place for a people who wanted to be near their deity in death – or perhaps it was for some other reason.

Aim for **Alsop**. You need to find a stile in the wall at the bottom of the fifth field. Climb this and walk towards the gate in the bottom left corner of the field beyond. Walk straight down through the farm to the road at the bottom. (³/₄ mile)

⑫ Turn right along the road, visiting the church en route. As you come back to the road from the church there's a good view of the Hall. Continue along the lane. When it bends right, take the path on the left. Walk up the right side of the field and 30 yards before the wood cross the stile on the right. Continue uphill to cross a squeezer leading up to the Trail. You pass a seat in memory of Greenlow Jasper. Turn left on the Trail to return to the start. (¹/₂ mile)

Date walk completed:

MINNINGLOW, THE HIGH PEAK TRAIL AND PARWICH

ROYSTONE GRANGE

Distance:
8¹/₄ miles
(5 miles to
the Sycamore)

Starting point:
*Minninglow car
park near Pikehall.
GR 194582*

Map: OS Outdoor Leisure 24 The Peak District – White Peak Area

How to get there: *From Pikehall on the A5012
between Newhaven and Grangemill turn south for Parwich.
Turn left for the car park just over ¹/₂ mile later.*

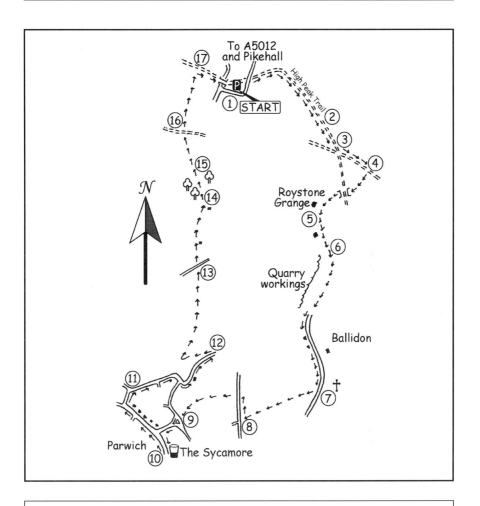

A walk through history with Minninglow and Roystone Grange (with its Romano-British period walls) featuring heavily – and that's just the first mile or so. This is another area that's not as popular as some others nearby but that's an advantage because the peace and quiet will be more noticeable, especially when you've left the High Peak Trail behind you. The route continues past Ballidon's church in a field to the lunch stop at Parwich and then returns northwards on cross-country paths.

The **Sycamore Inn** is the only pub in Parwich so if it's closed or you're running (sorry walking) late you've got problems. There is, however, a shop in the village, which you will pass later. So what about the Sycamore! It's a friendly pub popular with walkers and cyclists, and good tasty food is the rule of the day, with items such as home-made steak pie as well as sausage and egg with salad garnish being on offer. There are also sandwiches and salads as well as specials such as Cajun Butterfly Chicken. The beers are all Robinson's – Old Tom, for instance, with seasonal brews such as Robin Bitter and Cumbria Way.

The opening times are from 12 noon until 2 pm on weekdays and until 3 pm at weekends. Food is available until 1.45 pm. You should phone to check the evening times, if you need them.

Telephone: *01335 390212.*

The Walk

① From the car park, walk eastward along the **High Peak Trail**, crossing the lane almost immediately. Tree-topped **Minninglow** should be visible to your right very soon, being higher than anything else around. (1 mile)

② A mile after leaving the car park, pass an old quarry on your left. Just beyond take care (especially of children and dogs) on the embankment. There's quite a drop on both sides. Beyond is an old limekiln on the left. **Minninglow** by now is also to your left. (¹/₄ mile)

③ **Gallowlow Lane** crosses the Trail at an angle. Turn left along this old road. Because it's a 'road' you could meet anything – horses, 4x4s, motorbikes. (¹/₄ mile)

④ After 400 yards climb the stile on your right. Walk down the field, passing under the Trail. Beyond this descend into the bottom corner of the field, negotiating a squeezer stile to the right of the water trough. Proceed down the left side of the next field to cross a step-stile. **Roystone Grange** is ahead. As you cross this stile look back to your right. A round-roofed building is an old explosives store. Head down the track, continuing for 70 yards down the right side of a second field. Cross a stile, heading half left across a small field. (¹/₂ mile)

⑤ On the track beyond turn left. The route takes you through the left-hand of two gates.

Take the gate on the right to reach an interpretation board on the chapel-like pumping station. To the right of this is where the medieval grange used to be. A 'dig' took place a few years ago which unearthed its foundations.

Returning to the route, pass through the left-hand gate. Follow the track down the valley. Signs state that blasting takes place between the hours of 9 and 5. Get ready to duck! (1/4 mile)

Where the valley opens out look out on the left for the remains of five or six walls built nearly 2,000 years ago. All that can be seen now are vague mounds running directly up the valley side from the track, the 'bumps' being embedded with a line of stones here and there. These ancient walls were researched by Martin Wildgoose some years ago. In the next field, though, there is no sign of these walls.

⑥ Stay on the main track, ignoring others to left and right. Suddenly, you turn a corner and the modern world intrudes in the form of quarry buildings. After crossing a cattle grid, take the lower road. Pass the

quarry workings on your right. Stay on the road to reach the hamlet of **Ballidon**. Keep on the road as it bears round to the right. Stay on it until you see **All Saints' church** on your left in the field. There is a stile (with a concrete path leading up to the church) on your left as you near the church. (1½ miles)

All Saints' church is much older than it looks. It was restored in the early 19th century but it dates to Norman times. It is unusual to have a church or chapel in the middle of the field. It is always possible, of course, that originally there was a village nearer to it.

⑦ Just 30 yards beyond the stile on your left, turn right over the stile taking you onto the **Limestone Way** with its ram's head logo. Walk up the right side of the field beyond.

SYCAMORE INN, PARWICH

Cross a footbridge at the far end. In the second field, head half left, just to the right of the far left corner. Keep forward just to the left of the far left corner in the third field. After crossing a slab-bridge, head up the right side of the field ahead, veering slightly left at the end to the stile by the gate. (1/2 mile)

⑧ Turn right up the lane for 300 yards. Just before the road levels out, take the path on the left. Walk down the left side of three fields, one after the other, to reach the far left corner of the third. Climb some steps. Bear left to reach a stile. Walk straight through a couple of paddocks to come out on the road beside **Stubley** on your right. (1/2 mile)

⑨ Ignore the road to the left. Walk forward, taking the second left, and 30 yards later turn right along the road beside the churchyard. Pass the green on the right to reach a T-junction. Turn left to the **Sycamore**. (1/4 mile)

⑩ After lunch, turn right along the road used earlier. Don't turn right by the green, but stay on the main road which is signed '**Alsop**' and '**Newhaven**'. Subsequently ignore the left turn for **Alsop**. Follow the road round to the right near the shop (signed '**Newhaven**') and 75 yards later turn right along the short walled path to rise up to a lane beyond. (1/4 mile)

⑪ Turn right along the lane. Ignore a footpath on the left to reach what used to be **Parwich Care Centre** above to your left. Keep forward here, ignoring a lane dropping downhill, sharp right. The lane you're on is shown as a cul-de-sac but you can walk it. On reaching **Lea House** ignore the path forking left uphill; take the track ahead marked 'Unsuitable for Motors'. Follow this as it descends to another lane. Turn left here and follow it round a tight left bend. Pass **Littlewood Farm**. (1/2 mile)

⑫ About 200 yards later turn sharp left over a stile into the woodland. Follow this path for approximately 180 yards until it joins another path descending from the right. Turn right here and negotiate what can sometimes be a slippery hillside. After 100 yards, the path comes out of the trees. Keep in the same direction through the hawthorns to reach a wall corner on your left. Bear slightly left here, walking almost parallel to the wall on your left to cross a stile 60 yards later. Go over the field beyond to a stile 20 yards to the left of the far right corner. Head *slightly* left across the next field. Keep forward in the subsequent field, with a wall on your right, and 450 yards later you reach a lane. (3/4 mile)

⑬ Cross this to a stile beside the gate opposite. Walk towards a stile in the wall in front of the stone building ahead. Beyond this, walk alongside the wall on your right, passing the outbuilding as you go. Squeeze through a stile in the far right corner to enter a third field. At the far end of this third field cross the stile on your right. Descend towards **Lowmoor Farm** in the valley. Cross the wall and walk up the left side of the large, low building. Pass a pond to your left and keep forward to a stile 20 yards ahead. Cross this and bear left on the track beyond. ($^1/_2$ mile)

⑭ Stay on the track, leaving the trees. Ignore a gate on the left. Head towards a stile 20 yards to the right of the gate in front. Beyond this head for the gateway at the right side of the plantation ahead. Pass through the left hand of two gates beyond this. Head towards the trees in front, walking alongside a wall on your right to get there. Stay in the same direction out of the trees to reach a stile. ($^1/_4$ mile)

⑮ Cross this, heading forward in the general direction of some trees jutting out $^1/_2$ mile in front of you. Cross a couple of tumbled-down walls, then a third poor wall by a couple of gateposts. Climb a stile in the gateway ahead, crossing the narrow field beyond. Cross another stile to walk beside a wall on your right to reach a track. ($^1/_2$ mile)

⑯ Cross the stile in front. Walk to another just left of the *nearest* gate across the field. In field 2 bear slightly right to the stile to the right of the trees ahead. Head in a similar direction to the far right corner of field 3 to cross a stile beside a gate. This takes you through a plantation. Enter the field beyond and walk on the left side of the wall running away from you. Follow this all the way to a stile leading you onto the Trail. ($^1/_2$ mile)

The High Peak Trail continues northwards to Friden and then on to Parsley Hay. At Friden, beside the brickworks, there are some interpretation panels explaining how the brickworks operated there. Beyond Parsley Hay the Trail continues as far as Dowlow at present.

⑰ Turn right here back to the car. ($^1/_2$ mile)

Date walk completed:

WINSTER, IBLE AND BONSALL

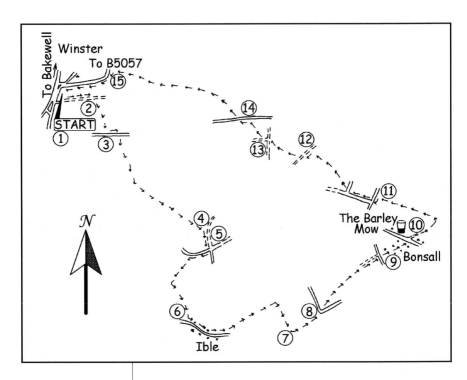

Distance:
9 miles
(5¼ miles to
the Barley Mow)

Starting point:
*West Bank car park,
Winster.
GR 239602*

Map: OS Outdoor Leisure 24 The Peak District – White Peak Area

How to get there: *Winster is reached on the B5057 or
the B5056 south of Bakewell. Approaching from the east,
drive along the main street and as the road bears right,
turn sharp left uphill. At the top of the hill the car park is
on your left. There is room for parking on the road
thereabouts too.*

A FIELD ON THE WAY TO BONSALL – FOR CENTURIES A SITE OF LEAD MINING

*W*inster and Bonsall and the land between are riddled with lead mine shafts. This walk crosses ground that has been plundered for years and a fascinating route it is. On the first stretch you visit Ible, an out of the way village if ever there was. On the way back you get a piggyback on the Limestone Way and, all in all, you'll have a satisfying day out discovering a few paths you've probably never used before.

The **Barley Mow** in Bonsall is a great place, full of photographs of local characters, and full of different bits and pieces that you could spend hours studying. It's a small pub so try and get there in good time.

The food is 'Traditional English Cooking' and according to the landlord, 'Most of the food is made here.' I can certainly vouch for the cheese and onion pie! The beers are Hardys & Hansons, Hartington Bitter and Abbot Ale plus a guest such as Timothy Taylor Landlord. Opening times are 6 pm until 11 pm on Monday to Friday, 12 noon until 11 pm on Saturday and 12 noon until 10.30 pm on Sunday. That's right – the pub isn't open in the daytime during the week. A good alternative is the King's Head, also in Bonsall. Telephone: 01629 822703.

For further details about the Barley Mow visit their website: www.barleymowbonsall.co.uk. The landlord has asked me to mention that if you've got your GPS with you the Barley Mow is at GR SK27555-58054.

Telephone: *01629 825685.*

 *The Walk*

① From the car park, turn left up the road, passing **The Old Parish Poorhouse**. Keep left at the main road. With the **Lead Ore House** to your right, turn left along the **Limestone Way**. There are wide ranging views to your left. (¹/₂ mile)

The Lead Ore House was like a night safe. Lead miners could deposit their ore there overnight.

② After 400 yards, turn right through a squeeze-stile. Head 40 yards beyond the gap in the wall to your left. Keep in the same direction in fields 2 and 3, passing through a squeeze-stile by a gateway in the latter. Walk down to the bottom left corner of field 4 to a road. (¹/₄ mile)

③ Turn left and 150 yards later turn right over a stile. Walk down the first field to a squeeze-stile 250 yards ahead (ignoring a path to the left). Bear slightly left in the second field to another stile. Walk along the bottom side of the next two fields. Aim just left of the far right corner of field 5, continuing to the far right corner of field 6. Pass through a stile and turn left. Walk alongside the wall on your left through the next seven fields. Some of the squeeze-stiles are very narrow. (1¹/₄ miles)

④ Turn right along a rough track. It's a 'road' so be prepared to meet vehicles.

After 50 yards there's a capped lead mine shaft on your left – evidence of man's impact on this landscape, which has taken quite a battering over the years. To your right, stone is still being ripped out of the earth in the large quarry at Grange Mill.

Pass **Whitelow Farm** on your left and continue for 150 yards. (¹/₄ mile)

⑤ Turn right at the crossroads.

Follow the lane until it bends sharp right. Just round the corner, pass through a wicket gate on your left. Walk down to the middle of the bottom wall. Cross a stile just beyond it in the fence. Keep in the same direction, passing through another squeeze-stile, with a wicket gate immediately beyond. Head towards the ruined building 80 yards ahead. On reaching it, turn left uphill, passing through another wicket gate in the fence. Keep forward to the far end of the field ahead. Pass through another wicket gate just beyond a tumbled-down wall. Bear slightly right to a tumbled-down stile. Turn right on the track beyond. (¹/₂ mile)

⑥ Turn left into **Ible** (rhymes with 'bible'). Pass **Chestnut Farm**, dated 1736. Pass the water troughs on your left. Head out of **Ible**. As the road levels take the path on your left. Cut the corner of the field beyond. Keep in the same direction in field 2, passing through a stile at the top of the field. Cross narrow field 3, keeping forward through fields 4 to 9. In field 10 head forward, keeping to the left of the hedge jutting out ahead. Cross the stile and turn left. Walk along the left side of fields 11 and 12, continuing forward on the right side of 13. After 50 yards turn right through the stile and descend parallel to

the wall on your right. Continue in this direction through fields 14 and 15, heading into the bottom right corner of field 16. Keep down the right side of field 17 and negotiate another stile. (1 mile)

⑦ Beyond this (with a track descending more steeply ahead of you – **Hollowchurchway**) turn left alongside the wall on your left. With an outbuilding on your left, bear half right to reach a wall corner. Turn left alongside the wall.

Mountain Cottage is half right of you across the valley. D.H. Lawrence lived here for a short time. The landlord at the Barley Mow says that Lawrence wrote a short story about Ible.

Pass a gap in the wall. At the end of the wall, walk forward for 50 yards before bearing half left towards a stile 200 yards ahead. This brings you to a lane. (¹/₂ mile)

THE LEAD ORE HOUSE, WINSTER

⑧ Cross to the stile opposite. Walk forward for 10 yards. Bear half right across the pockmarked field ahead and 300 yards later you reach a wall corner. Bear right, keeping the wall on your right. Almost immediately you drop down into, and then out of, a rake. After 100 yards you reach a sqeeze-stile. Pass through this, keeping forward alongside the wall ahead.

Crich Stand (above a quarry) may be visible in the distance.

Walk beside the wall in the second field, keeping forward at the wall corner through the stile ahead. Cross field 3 to another stile, then cross the corner of field 4 (yes, there is a stile there). The path is obvious in field 5. On entering a narrow sixth field, turn left to a gate. Turn right down the track beyond. (³/₄ mile)

⑨ At the road, cross to the double gates, walking down the track beyond. Keep to the right of the breeze-block buildings in the farmyard. Just beyond the second one pass through a squeeze-stile, heading downhill to the tarmac 'path'. Descend to reach the **Barley Mow**. (¹/₄ mile)

⑩ From the pub, turn left, pass the 'Gents' and immediately ascend the tarmac lane on your left. Continue, ignoring a path sharp left and keeping to the left of the unusual

shaped house. Head forward to a farmgate, ignoring a grass left fork. Pass through a stile by the gate. Walk diagonally across the field beyond, keeping in the same direction in the second field. Enter a third field, turning left to reach a walled path off to the left after 20 yards. To reach the **King's Head**, turn right down the walled path to reach the pub at the bottom of the hill. Follow this through to **Uppertown**, ignoring a path to the left as you proceed. Keep in the same direction through the houses to reach **Uppertown Lane** (a T-junction). (¹/₂ mile)

⑪ Turn left, then almost immediately right. Pass **Hollies Farm**. Turn right along **Abel Lane**. Almost immediately pass through a squeeze-stile on the left. Cross the field, aiming for a stile 50 yards behind the house. Bear slightly right in field 2, heading just right of the building in field 3. Bear left in field 4, passing the building on your left (ignore a path forking right). Keep on the left side of field 5. In field 6 the path splits; keep forward, ignoring the left fork, along the **Limestone Way** to a walled path. (³/₄ mile)

⑫ Turn left and 250 yards later pass through a squeeze-stile on the right. Keep on the right side of the first field, bearing slightly left in field 2. Keep in the same direction in field

3. Cross narrow field 4. Bear left in field 5 alongside the left-hand boundary. Where this bears left, keep forward to the stile ahead. Views of the **Dark Peak** lie to your right and **Chatsworth** should be visible. In field 6 keep in the same direction to the stile ahead. ($^1/_2$ mile)

⑬ At the track turn right for 30 yards, then left, then almost immediately right. Head diagonally across the field. Bear slightly left across the next field towards the gap in the wall. Stay in this direction in field 3, aiming for the 'bumps' on the far side. Pass through a stile into field 4 and cut the corner, bearing slightly right in field 5 and passing a wall corner jutting into the field as you go. This brings you to the road. ($^1/_4$ mile)

⑭ Turn left for 50 yards. Cross the stile on the right. Walk diagonally across the large field, keeping just right of the double electricity poles. Walk directly across the second field. Bear slightly right across field 3, keeping in the same direction in field 4. Cut the corner of field 5, proceeding in the same direction in field 6 to the wall at the bottom.

Bear left beside this in fields 7, 8 and 9, heading towards **Luntor Rocks**, surrounded by trees. Partway along field 9 cross the stile on your right, continuing beyond with the wall/fence on your left. Pass the **Rocks** on your left. Pass through a wicket gate. Keep forward to a stone squeeze-stile standing forlornly in the middle of the field. Walk beyond this to another stile, **Winster** now being visible ahead. Cross the stile, keeping on the right side of the wall in front. Pass through a gap, heading forward along a steadily descending path. On reaching a 3 ft high stone beneath the beech trees, bear half right over the field beyond. Pass through another gap, walking on the top side of the field towards a squeeze-stile. This takes you on a grassy path, with a garden below to your right. Walk between the house walls to a lane. ($1^1/_4$ miles)

⑮ Turn half left uphill, passing **Rose Cottage** and then **Oak Lea**. Stay on this road all the way back to the car park and pass various interesting properties, the last one being **Pinfold Cottage** on your left. ($^1/_2$ mile)

Date walk completed: